Book of... ...Righteous Survival EMP Saga

By: Timothy A. Van Sickel

4/14/17

To Charlotte

I hope you enjoy this tale.

Tim Van Sickel

Property of:
Charlotte Reed
820 Locust Ave
Manchester, PA 17345

All rights resevred

Copyright 2016 Timothy A Van Sickel

Original and modified cover art by Luz Adriana Villa and CoverDesignStudio.com

Dedicated to my Lord and Savior, Jesus Christ, who inspired me, and my wife and family who encouraged me.

Table of Contents

Contents

Author's Foreword		5
Roster of main characters		6
Trigger Warning!		7
Chapter 1	I Knew, September, 2018	8
Chapter 2	No Plan, September 11. 2018	12
Chapter 3	The Funeral Late July, 2011	23
Chapter 4	Gathering, September 11, 2018	29
Chapter 5	Getting Janie, September 11, 2018	35
Chapter 6	Electricity, June, 2016	48
Chapter 7	Activated, September 11, 2018	53
Chapter 8	The Kids, September 11, 2018	62
Chapter 9	Bacon, Spring 2014	74
Chapter 10	First Night, September 11, 2018	78
Chapter 11	Second Morning, Farmstead, September 12, 2018	88
Chapter 12	Second Morning, Central City, September 12, 2018	93
Chapter 13	Hunting, November 2008	102
Chapter 14	Moxham Burning, September 12, 2018	109
Chapter 15	Returning Home, September 12, 2018	115
Chapter 16	Security, 2015	133
Chapter 17	Getting Home, Part 2, September 12, 2018	136
Chapter 18	Back Home, September 12, 2018	141
Chapter 19	Moxham, Day 2, Herc's Story, September 12, 2018	152
Chapter 20	Wagerly's Compound, Day 2, September 12, 2018	157
Chapter 21	Moxham, Night 2, Herc's Story, September 12, 2018	162
Chapter 22	3rd Morning, Farmstead, September 13, 2018	165
Chapter 23	Central City, Day 3, September 13. 2018	176
Chapter 24	More Central City, Day 3, September 13, 2018	189
Chapter 25	Moxham to Davidsville, Day 3 Herc's Story, September 13, /2018	194
Chapter 26	Home Again, September 13, 2018	202
Chapter 27	Wagerlys' Compound, September 13, 2018	218
Chapter 28	Wagerlys' Compound, September 14, 2018	220
Chapter 29	Farmstead, Day 4, September 14, 2018	222
Chapter 30	Day 4 Herc to Central City, September 14, 2018	233
Final words		254

Author's Foreword

I have read many series about the collapse of the Western World; every scenario from mutant viruses causing zombie-like uprisings, EMP attacks causing the collapse of the grid, to general economic collapse due to bad policies. I have even read part of a romance series set during an EMP-type collapse. I have felt that all of these series of novels have lacked one very important aspect--religion--or a religious morality.

This series of books follows a man, his family, and surrounding community, through a devastating EMP attack on America. The man happens to be a born-again Christian who tries to follow his moral compass at every twist and turn. He has brought up his family to be God-loving Christians, willing to help out their fellow man, if at all possible. And he associates and surrounds himself with like-minded people.

Setting priorities, and following what he believes to be right through the eyes of his morality, is what sets this series apart from others like it. Ninety percent of Americans believe in God. Seventy-seven percent of Americans say they are Christians. Twenty-five percent of Americans say they are Evangelical Christians. In rural America, I assume that number is higher.

So how will Christians deal with a collapse scenario? That is the question that this series of novels tries to portray. I am not a scholarly priest. I am not a survival specialist. I am neither a farmer nor a gun expert. But I truly felt called by God to write this novel as a Christian man who does think a collapse of some type may occur.

The people in this novel are fictional characters. Any resemblance to real people is strictly coincidental. I live in Johnstown, Pennsylvania, where the story is based, and the towns and places do exist or are loosely based on real places. I hope you find what unfolds on the following pages to be exciting, intriguing, entertaining, and in some ways uplifting.

Roster of Main Characters

Surival of a societal collapse event will require like minded people gathering together. Therefore, this book has a significant number of characters. Hopefully this roster will help you in understanding the relationships of the main characters.

Mark and Rebecca Mays
    Melonie & Brad, Brit & Kennie, Zach & Janie

    Zach and Janie
        Rusty, Blake, James (Jimmy), Mark, Sarah

    Brit and Kennie (Ken)
        Larson, Grace

Rocco and Katie (Janie's parents)

Paul and Eve Mays (Mark's brother and sister in law)

John and Jan Mays (Mark's brother and sister in law)

Linc and Kim (travelers accepted in to the farmstead)

Thad   Local Farmer

Jerry   Local Deacon, Central City

Chris Speigle   Fire Chief, Hooversville

John Fisher   Army Ranger First Sergeant (retired), Central City

Herc, Leesa, John Jr.   Mark's employee and family

Frank Wagerlys   Head drug dealer

Hairy   Frank's Leiutenant

Trigger Warning!

ALERT! ALERT! ALERT!

PROCEED WITH CAUTION!

This novel contains characters that are openly religious. Their actions, words and thoughts are based in their Christian faith. In this novel people pray, and even quote scripture. The characters try to follow their Christian principles in dealing with very difficult decisions. They try to follow a moral code based on biblical teachings. If you find this offensive, you may not want to read this novel. You will also find minor swearwords and slightly objectionable language in order to keep the story real.

Chapter 1   I Knew, September, 2018

A sense of normalcy and peace returned to our mountain-top neighborhood… that is how I hope this story ends. Here is how it begins. I knew right away. There was no wondering, no second thoughts, no confusion. I knew immediately that bad things had happened; the world had changed.

I was sitting on a split-log bench by the chicken coop, looking out over our farmstead, enjoying the day, enjoying the beautiful creation we call earth. And then everything changed in an instant. The first thing I did was pray.

Earlier that morning I had checked on a renovation project one of my crews was working on in Davidsville. The job would wrap up in the next few days. My lead carpenter gave me a list of items we would need to finish up the small details. Paying attention to the details is the difference between a repeat customer or just another job completed. Going that extra bit means repeat business and referrals. It also gives you the satisfaction of knowing you did your best. I always try to do my best.

Then I had stopped to meet with a woman who was looking to renovate her patio area to incorporate a small pavilion with an outdoor kitchen. She had seen one we did on Benshoff Hill, and the extra effort on that job was now paying off.

I was taking the rest of day off, which means a day off the job site, working on proposals and taking care of paperwork, the insurances, permits, making sure we complied with all the newest regulations, researching products, etc. So I was back at my property. My wife had told me about a hole in the chicken coop, so I had repaired it before heading to the office to design the pavilion/kitchen. It's a constant effort to keep the coyotes, foxes and fisher cats away from the chickens and ducks.

I sat there smoking a cigarette, one of my bad habits left over from when I had a lot of bad habits. I was casually looking at the contrails in the sky above me. There were three of them, not uncommon in the skies of western Pennsylvania, mostly jets heading out of or into the Washington and Baltimore area airports. It was a beautiful day with clear blue skies. The goldenrod were brilliant at the edge of the pasture, and the chickens were still fussing from me working on the fence. I noticed a couple of redwing blackbirds dipping and dodging along the fenceline. It was the kind of day that I thank God for. But then, it wasn't.

One of the contrails puffed, puffed again then sputtered and disappeared. I immediately noticed that the other two did the same, their contrails showing a distress in their flight. And I knew what had happened, no second thoughts, no confusion. I pulled out my cell phone from my pocket, dead, confirmation. September 11, 2018.

Transfixed, I continued to watch the sky as three small silver specks headed towards earth; the dead airplanes succumbing to gravity. I began to pray for those on board, as I knew they were tragically and frantically dealing with the inevitable. I prayed that they knew Jesus and were saved. I prayed that their hearts would be comforted in knowing their salvation even in the face of death.

Then I wondered, "Is this it? Is this Armageddon? Is this the Rapture? Am I going to see the face of God? Am I going to see the golden streets of heaven?" I have not always been a Christian but I rededicated myself to the Lord many years ago, and believe fully that I am saved through Christ's blood and God's grace.

So I continued to pray, asking for forgiveness, and thanking God for blessing my life as he has, praying for my children and grandchildren, and humanity as a whole. And I watched as the goldenrod swayed in the breeze, and the redwinged blackbirds flitted about, and the three silver specks plummeted to earth, growing in size as they rapidly neared their inevitable fate.

And I waited. For the Rapture. For the heavenly choirs. For the pearly gates. For the streets of gold. I waited to see the face of Jesus, my savior! And I watched the swaying goldenrod, the redwinged blackbirds, the clucking chickens, and the white clouds against a clear blue sky; and the dim fireball on the horizon as a silver speck disappeared over the far mountain treeline.

This ended my prayers and began a bit of panic. I'm still here. No golden streets, no face of God, no heavenly chorus. Did I get something wrong? Is my heart not pure enough? Was it all a myth? "No!" I cried out loud. "God, please forgive me for anything I have done against your will! Please forgive me for not following you, as I should, for straying from the path you wanted me to follow! Dear God, may your grace and forgiveness be upon me in Christ's name I do pray!" I wept.

But there I was, with the blue skies and billowing clouds, the swaying goldenrod, the blackbirds diving and dodging, the chickens still clucking and scratching. And I prayed again, this time for my wife, my children and grandchildren, and all of God's people. I prayed that I was not pure of heart but that they were. That they were seeing the golden streets, joining the heavenly choirs and fully experiencing the love of our Lord and savior, Jesus Christ.

The BOOM from the explosion over the horizon, where one of the plummeting airplanes had turned into a fireball, ended my prayers. I was still here, no Rapture, at least not for me. And I knew what had happened. Life on earth had just changed in ways no one could predict, but some of us had prepared for, including my family and me. We had been hit with an EMP, Electro-Magnetic Pulse, and anything with electronic circuitry was dead. Grid down, computers down, most vehicles dead, transportation systems grinding to a halt, factories, hospitals, grocery stores, modern farms, all shut down in one terrible instant.

    Was it an attack? Was it a sun flare? Doesn't matter I suppose. But life just radically changed for all of humanity.

Chapter 2   No Plan, September 11. 2018

It is time to start moving. No more contemplation and prayer. Three minutes past EMP, and there is no time to waste. Chaos is no more than 48 hours away, maybe less. I have to bring my loved ones home. My beautiful wife, my kids, my grandkids; those I can help that is, those here in the mountains of western Pennsylvania. My family is far flung, brothers and sisters as close as Pittsburgh and as far away as the west coast, and a stepdaughter in the Rocky Mountains with her husband and two sons.

We had all talked about something like this casually, maybe too casually. And we had all agreed that the farmstead would be our safe place. But I'm very worried that our plans are way too casual. Bringing my family home is going to be a challenge. Just finding my family is going to be a challenge!

I'm still in shock, semi-panic. I know what I saw, what has happened. My closest loved ones are all in town, twenty miles away. How many stalled cars, accidents, fires, panicked civilians, panicked police officers, are between them and me? How am I going get them home? What am I going to have to do to get them home?

I need to find my wife first. Her office is on the outskirts of town. She is way smarter than me in many ways and, as always, she will be the rock that will pull us all together. She is tall and has exotic mixed-race beauty, with emerald green eyes, but her troubled life, coming to age as a mixed-race woman, long before that was accepted, has given her common sense and compassion far beyond most people's ability to understand. Along with my faith, she will keep me grounded. My stepson and daughter-in-law live only a few miles further into town. They will be next, then their children. I'm going to have to wing it from there.

The chickens are clucking because of my sprint towards the house. The blackbirds scoot to the other end of the meadow. My dogs start barking and bouncing as if it's time to play. "No play time now my friends," I say as I make a mental list of what to bring, what I may encounter. Weapons, water, cash and first aid are what keep recurring in my mind.

I step in the door and grab the keys for the old van, then head towards the barn. I glance at the cluster of windmills on the nearby ridge top, the blades slowly turning in the morning breeze. "How long before those towering hulks begin to fall apart?" I wonder out loud. The circuitry controlling the pitch and direction of the blades is surely fried, the automatic shutdown system is fried. Without the control systems, the towering beasts are useless, and in the next big storm will spin out of control and literally fly apart.

My own small wind turbine is dutifully spinning away, generating electricity. Hopefully the Faraday cage surrounding the powerhouse, with all its control systems and batteries, that my brother Paul designed, has worked. I'll find out soon enough.

The barking dogs bring me back to my mission. I think about chaining the dogs, but decide to let them roam free under the circumstances. They are going to be my security until we get back. Pulling open the sliding barn doors, I run past my big Dodge 4x4 and say a silent prayer that the old van will start.

We have a 1978 Econoline van with a good drivetrain that I bought cheap a few years ago. My stepson and I put in new brake lines, did a front end rebuild, and some bodywork. Four new tires, and she was good for the road. We needed the big van to go anywhere with all the grandkids. We had just used it last week to take the kids out to the Juniata River to go fishing. When I bought it, I knew it was pre-electronics, EMP-proof. I even talked my wife out of a newer model, but I never brought up the EMP aspect.

I open the door and the dome light comes on! Hallelujah! Jumping in I turn the ignition and the old engine starts right up. I back her up the driveway to the side of the house where I can load up for this trip to town. It's going to be like no other trip before. Weapons, water, cash, first aid.

As I go back in the house I try a few light switches hoping the battery backup system has kicked in. The new house is wired for general power failure, which is common this far up the mountain. The control system and grid interface electronics are in the powerhouse Faraday cage, so I am hopeful. But no luck there. "Shit," I think, "did the Faraday cage fail? Not good." I pull open a few curtains to let some more light in as I head to my office.

I open an ordinary looking closet and unlock the heavy door. In my prep days, I couldn't afford a large enough gun safe so I settled for a closet built of doubled and overlapped 2" x 8"s, covered with ½" cement board and finished to look like an ordinary closet. Secure enough against the average crook, semi-fire resistant and a lot cheaper than a safe of the same size.

I set aside my two AR15s and load eight magazines for them. I also load three more magazines for my Glock and four for my wife's. Thinking of the urban terrain I'm heading into I also grab the Remington 870 12 gauge and a box of #4 along with my wife's Glock and her shoulder holster.

It's an awkward load to carry it all out to the van, but I get it there. I stash the ARs in the back of the van, and grab a blanket to wrap the Remington to hide it, because I want it in the front seat with me. I put my wife's Glock and spare ammo in the glove compartment, and stick my spare ammo in the door pocket. I make a quick check to make sure my Glock is still secure in my belt holster. It's kind of a habit.

Returning to the house, I head to the basement and grab a couple cases of water. I'm not sure why I need cases of water, but something in the back of my head says I should take it. I am sure it is God talking to me, preparing me for what is ahead.

Yes, God talks to me, and I talk to him, often. It's not a Charleston Heston in "Exodus" kind of thing where God speaks in a bold confident voice. More of a "hey Mark, take some water, you may need it" whisper. I think he talks to all of us everyday like that, we just don't hear it or ignore it. Think of the skits with a devil on one shoulder and an angel on the other. I try to listen to that angel, he's usually right.

Carrying the cases of water up the stairs, I stop at the bathroom and grab one of our first aid kits, and then head out to the van. Cash, I need cash too. I go back to the safe and grab $2,500 in hundreds and fifties. If anything is open, it will be cash only. If I have the opportunity or the need, I'll have the cash. After loading that, I go back in and secure the house. Locking the doors is all I can do; the security system is fried.

I jump in the van and check the gas, full. I fueled up on the way home from the Juniata. Time to head into town; a trip to town like no other trip I have ever taken.

***

It's a few hundred yards from my house to the edge of the property, then another quarter mile on our driveway, a country lane through my neighbor's farm until I hit the paved county road. It's still a beautiful day with clear blue skies. My blackbird friends have returned, and are skittering along the fence line. Our hay fields are ripe and ready for another mowing, my neighbor's corn is tall and ready for harvest.

Did I really see three planes drop from the sky? Was America really hit with a massive EMP? It is all so quiet and peaceful. Another picturesque day in the mountains of western Pennsylvania. I could take a picture right now, and it could appear on countless calendars and be subtitled "Harvest Time in the Laurel Highlands." It is truly surreal.

But I know what I saw, and I know what happened. I don't need some squelching noise and an emergency broadcast to come over a radio that doesn't work to confirm it. As I get closer to town, the devastation will begin to confirm what I already know.

I take a right heading off the mountain towards the little town of Central City. This high in the mountains, the few homes and farms are almost completely surrounded by state game lands and state forest. The houses I do pass show no signs of activity, the owners probably stuck at work or in town. About two miles down the road I encounter my first obstacle. It happens to be Thad Jones, on his old John Deere, moving his hay baler down the road to another hay field he leases as part of his dairy operation. Being the first person I have seen since the world changed, I have to stop and see what he knows.

"Hey Thad, did you see those planes go down?" I ask.

"What planes?" he asks. "I seen some planes earlier. Probably bringing the DC bigwigs in to spout off over at that dang Memorial ceremony thing. But nothin' other than that."

"That Memorial ceremony just went to crap," I say. "We been attacked again and 9/11 just got a hell of a lot worse. Check your cell phone, Thad. It's dead, and so is everything else electronic. I watched three planes nose dive. Big fireball and boom over towards Pleasantville. There are hundreds of pits in the ground all over this country now, just like Shanksville."

16

"Huh?" Thad responds. Looking at his cell phone he says, "You're right, it's dead. What do you mean we been attacked?"

"I ain't got much time, Thad, but someone nuked us and it fried everything electronic, cars, planes, computers. You name it, if it's got electronics, it's probably broke. Where's your wife?"

"She went in to see her Mom at the home, like every Tuesday," Thad responds.

"Go back home and drop the baler. Get some cash and head in to pick up her up. While you're there, buy anything you think you may need. You ain't going to be able to buy nothin' in a few days. Sounds weird, but buy salt, canning jars, spices, bleach, first aid stuff. I know it sounds crazy, but it's true. You'll see. You won't have no lights when you get home. Say a prayer, brother; this is going to get bad. I'm heading into Johnstown for the wife and kids."

"Shit, you ain't shittin' me, are you?"

"No, no I'm not," I say grimly as I pull off.

As I drive off, I think to myself that Thad is a devout Catholic, never misses mass, always volunteering for the fish fries and annual bazaar. It may be Armageddon, but no Rapture, I convince myself. A mile down the road I see a car, hood up, driver poking around at the engine hopelessly. I drive around him.

I pass three more cars like the first one before hitting the small town of Central City. A very small town, literally one light, not currently working, and a wreck. It's minor and I don't recognize the folks so I drive on. I have a more important mission, my wife, my kids, and my grandchildren.

I hit State Route 160 North. It's a sparsely traveled road, except for coal and logging trucks. It will take me through the remote hills and forests for the next ten miles. Then I'll get to Route 56, a four lane that will take me into Johnstown. I hit the pedal to the metal. Now that I'm off the county roads, I can start to put on some speed. But I have to quickly slow down as a log hauler is stalled in my lane and two pickups are on the left hand berm, stalled, hoods up, drivers looking confused. I keep going.

Driving a little slower, I pass several more stalled cars and trucks. One guy stuck in a ditch tries to flag me down, but I keep going. It causes a dilemma in my mind--I should stop and help. But I can't. I'll never reach Rebecca.

I see thick black smoke up ahead, oily and dark. It's too close to be from something in town, it has to be something bad on the road. I slow down a bit as I come up to a few sharper turns in the road. I see the source of the smoke, and it is bad. A coal truck couldn't make the turn at the same time as a car was coming the other way. It is not pretty. Car meets coal truck is never good. The truck is off the road and overturned, the car and truck are on fire, I don't see anyone. My heart aches as I drive on. I pray for their souls. I pray for forgiveness.

I travel several more miles. More dead vehicles and minor wrecks. I'm coming up on the intersection with the four lane. I slow down, expecting trouble. I expect that I'm going to have to dodge and go. I'm only a few miles from Becca's office now. Nothing is going to stop me.

At the intersection, cars and trucks east and west bound were stopped at the light, and sit dead where they were stopped. The north and southbound traffic on Route 160 did not fare as well. There is a serious head-on in the middle of the intersection. An overturned coal truck that couldn't make the turn is off the road, in the ditch. So are several cars and a pickup. There are flares out. People are trying to help the injured. There is no cop car present but there is a cop, trying his best to keep people calm and take control of the situation.

Everyone is startled as my big Dodge van rolls through the intersection. I dodge them and the wreck, and start to head westbound on four lane Route 56. Too late, the cop realizes a vehicle has pulled through his intersection, and with great agitation he runs towards me in my van, trying to stop me. But by this time I am heading west and he is in the rearview mirror. I keep rolling.

***

Rebecca's office is only three miles away. But in two miles I will start to hit a big shopping district with lots of traffic, people, and cops. Funny, I think, traffic will be stalled vehicles and bewildered people with agitated cops having no clue as to what has happened. No patrol car, no radio, no command system, and no word as to what has happened or what to do. As much as I respect law enforcement, in this situation, they could be the loose cannon that ends my world, literally. Dealing with them is going to be a big challenge. But I will do what I need to do to get my family back to the farmstead.

I see two Harley Davidsons heading east towards the mountains. Guy and a girl on each bike. They have saddlebags and bedrolls. I wonder if they know what's happened and are heading to a safe place. Or are they just getting out of town, fleeing the chaos to come? I wonder how many bikes are still running.

Heading up the hill towards the shopping district, it is almost impassable with stalled cars and confused commuters. I'm on the berm several times and almost have to run a few people over who are trying to stop me. Close to the top of the hill is a residential road I can take to bypass the shopping areas. I have to slow down to make the turn. The four-lane light must have been green because there is not a line of stalled traffic, but there are two wrecks and lot of people. I can tell there are several serious injuries from the condition of the cars and the grouping of the people, some kneeling down attending to the injured. Three guys try to stop me. They catch me by surprise because I am gawking at the wrecked cars. Before I can lay on the horn and speed up, they box me in. This is not good.

I hit the horn hard as I lean out the window and holler, "Outta my way, I got to pick up my wife and kids!" The three of them start heading towards my door. I move my hand to the pistol grip of my Glock.

As the first one reaches the door he pleads, "We gotta get my wife to the hospital, she's hurt real bad. The phones don't work, none of the cars will start, hardly anything is moving. You gotta help us!"

Unwittingly they have opened a path for me to get through. My heart breaking. I look at the distraught man and say, "I'm very sorry but I got to get my wife and kids." I lay on the horn and step on the gas as they jump from the sudden noise and movement. Turning on the side street, two of them chase after me shaking their fists. The third, the husband, falls to his knees, crying. I say a prayer for them, and me.

I ask God, "How can I do this? How can I save my family and ignore these people who are hurting? Am I going to lose my soul? Dear Lord, please forgive me." Even if I tried to help, it would be pointless. Getting to the hospital, which is all the way through town, would be almost impossible. And the hospital will be as disabled as everything else. The EMP will have fried all the modern medical equipment; even the backup systems and powerful modern generators will be fried. Many patients are dying right now, or dead. "Dear Lord, give me strength, that I may make it through this day. Grant me the wisdom to know when I can truly help or when I must move on. Be with us all as we face the challenges of this day," I pray out loud.

I am only a half-mile from Becca's office. But I have to pass a few busy streets, a couple of schools, where some of my grandkids are, and then the township office; and the township police department. Anxiety grows in my chest.

At the top of the hill is the secondary school. It looks like a fire drill. All the kids are out on the large lawns, grouped by classes, I guess. The teachers are trying to keep some semblance of order. The younger ones seem to be taking it in stride, sitting on the grass, talking amongst themselves. The older ones look to be getting restless after an hour with no explanation and no activity. The administrators, I assume, are gathered talking animatedly. Several turn and stare at me, some with bewilderment, as I drive past. I try to catch sight of my grandkids, but the crowd is too large, so I concentrate on what's ahead, the township building, the police department.

There are two cruisers in the parking lot with two officers and a couple of civilians. They are spread out along the sidewalk standing and kneeling over a bunch of equipment. I see two more civilians and another officer walk out the door with more equipment and boxes. I realize it's laptops and printers, communications gear and even fire extinguishers! Being too dark inside the building they are bringing it outside, trying to figure out what works and what doesn't.

Besides a few stalled cars, my path is clear. I step on the gas and make the turn towards Becca's office. This brings a reaction from the police as they see a working vehicle. I see one grab his radio, as if to call to someone, as they all start running towards me shouting. I have mobility on my side so I keep on going. Radio dude throws the radio down as he realizes his futility. The other two pull side arms and aim in my direction. Oh crap, I think.

21

But nothing happens. I am already out of range, and I have broken no laws, I don't think I have anyways. Not yet. I keep going.

As I pass the college, there are people all over the place, including on the road. But they move aside at my approach. Again I get the stares and some urgent waving and yelling, but I drive on. I have a mission. Wife, kids, grandkids.

Chapter 3   The Funeral   Late July, 2011

We buried my father today. Next to his wife of 62 years, in a family plot in Pittsburgh, near his aunt and uncle, and his parents. It was a sad day. It brought back memories of my mother as well as my father. I miss my mother, and now I will miss my father too. But they brought me up well, in the Church, and I will celebrate the good life they both led.

We have all returned back to my parent's farmstead in the Laurel Highlands. Even though it is a long trip from Pittsburgh and I am the only one who lives nearby, we have gathered at my folks "retirement" home, because we all now consider it home.

My folks moved here almost twenty years ago, before my dad actually retired. We all fell in love with the place. It is where we have celebrated holidays, gone hunting and fishing together, grew closer to each other, even though we were all grown and living our own lives by the time they moved here. My wife and I were even married here. We held the ceremony by the pond, and moved to the front lawn for the reception. Despite us all having been raised in Pittsburgh, going to the farm in the Laurel Highlands is really going home for us all.

It's a rather large gathering, my two brothers, my three sisters, their spouses, all our kids and grandkids. Add in a few remaining aunts and uncles, many cousins and many friends, both from Pittsburgh and Somerset, and there are over one hundred people here.

And we are here to celebrate a life well led. My father is in heaven now with the Father. And we all celebrate what a blessing he and my mother have been to so many people. Being brought up in a strong Christian family brings a different atmosphere to a funeral.

My oldest brother, Paul, rises and clamors for attention. "I want to thank you all for coming out and spending time with us here at Mountainside to celebrate the life my father led. It has been said you can tell a man's worth in life by the gathering at his death. And while we all will miss him, his legacy will be carried on by us all. The morals and values that he instilled in us, have been passed on to his many children and grandchildren, and have been spread not only across western Pennsylvania, but also from coast to coast.

"Dad taught us so much. Integrity. Selflessness. Independence. Humor. Compassion. But most of all, he taught us love. How to love and respect our wives, how to love our children, heck, if he managed to love us, we gotta be able to love our children!" A few snickers are heard around the crowd. "But seriously, most importantly, he taught us to love God and respect his Word. I think that is reflected in all who are here. We know he is in heaven, with Mom, smiling down on the legacy that they left behind together. I pray, literally, that we can follow in his footsteps. Again, thank you all for coming. Celebrate the legacy our father has left behind and celebrate the honest and generous life he led. Before we eat, Reverend Jones will say a blessing."

Reverend Jones stands, "Paul said it well, a man's worth can be judged by the offspring he produces. And in Peter's case, that is more than just his children, but also in the many lives he has effected. Let us thank God for the bounty he has provided us.

"Dear Lord, we thank you so much for allowing us to know Peter, a man who followed you daily and, like Peter of the Bible, truly built churches in honor of you and your love for us. Peter once told me that a parent's most important mission in life is to lead his children to Christ and life eternal. I believe Peter left this earth having completed his most important mission.

"Father, may you bless this gathering, that we may be nourished in spirit and may you bless this food that we may be nourished in strength and, like Peter, may we honor you in all we do. Amen."

As unofficial host, I rise and let everyone know to help themselves to the buffet and refreshments and thank them once again for coming to both mourn our loss and celebrate our father's life and legacy.

I sit with my wife Rebecca, Paul, John my other brother and their wives, Eve and Jan. John, always the tactful one says, "You know, Mark, this place is all yours in the will. Do you think you can handle it? Lotta land, lotta upkeep. Heck, me and Jan could move into the old farm house and help you out."

Jan quickly chimes in, "We're not moving way out here to the top of this mountain, a thousand miles from anything! I like it quite fine with neighbors I can see, and a store closer than five miles away! Besides, how would we ever visit the kids, it takes two hours just to get to the airport!"

"But Jan," John says, "we could be totally self sufficient! Raise some cows and pigs, get some chickens, plant corn, even barley and hops for some beer."

"Well, ya better plant some grape vines too because you're gonna need some pretty good wine to get me out here," Jan quips.

"Y'all are too much," I say. "But you are exactly right. Self sufficient living, that's how we're going to swing it. Rebecca and I are going to move our small operation out here. We already have ducks and the goat, we'll just expand a bit. And Thad down the road, he has always wanted to grow corn up here. I could lease him about sixty acres, that'll pay taxes and upkeep."

"You up for that, Becca?" asks Eve.

Becca responds, "I love my animals! So long as Mark takes care of what comes out the back end, I'll take care of what goes in the front end." That gets a good chuckle from everyone at the table.

"I don't know how that deal got started," I say, "but that seems to be the way it works. And they all love her and couldn't give a rat's ass about me! Go figure!"

We continue to talk of the farm and my parents and how they loved the outdoors. We talk of how much they taught us, from tying knots and cutting down trees to making jellies and canning venison. My dad loved red raspberries and blueberries. There is still a large patch of each that he tended out by the barn. We all got raspberry jam every year at Christmas. And if you were here on a Saturday morning, you got blueberry pancakes, just like when we were kids.

***

My youngest sister, Lessa, and her west coast husband, Josh, approach us along with their three teenage children. "Mark, you have to show us around! The kids have never been here in the summer and I don't think Josh and I have since Mom and Dad finished the house. It's absolutely beautiful with the trees so green and everything in bloom!"

"I'd love to, Les," I say. "I need to stretch my legs a bit anyway. Who's up for a nice walk?" My brothers and wife decline, enjoying the memories they are sharing.

As I rise, my oldest stepdaughter, Mellonie, and our son-in-law Brad, step up with their two kids. Brad is retired military. Having often been stationed overseas, they have only been here once, for the wedding. "We'd like the grand tour too, Mark. Come on Mom, show us around." Rebecca, not wanting to miss time with her kids and grandkids, agrees to go with us.

"We'll walk out the road to the old farm house and then swing down past the pond and back up around to here. That will give us a good walk without trekking too far or going off the path," I say as we start out.

Heading past the hundred and thirty year old barn, the grandkids pester to go inside. I show them the old tractor and a couple old farm implements. I point out the massive beams still holding the place together, forty-foot chestnuts, hand hewn. On the lower level I show them the stalls and feed troughs still in place, and the original stone foundation, recently repaired, that holds up the large structure. The kids want to climb to the hay loft and explore, but still being in good clothes, their parents shush them along, out the old rolling doors.

We walk past the raspberry patch, and I show them the large vegetable garden, idle this year because of Dad's poor health. Next is the blueberry patch and we stop long enough to pluck a few and pop them in our mouths, sweet and juicy!

We reach the old farmhouse, still in good repair, its chestnut framing holding up strong. It's just off from the property line, but still a quarter mile from the county road. It's typical of a nineteenth century farmhouse: two stories with an ell shape, kitchen in the rear, full front porch, three chimneys. It has newer vinyl siding but, thankfully, whoever did it made sure to maintain the classic architecture. Kids being kids, they want to climb the apple trees in the back yard, but again we shush them along.

We take a path to the left, skirting the neighbor's cornfield and head down towards the big spring-fed pond. Redwinged blackbirds and sparrows flit around the meadow to our right as we come up on the pond.

"Look along the edge of the water, kids," I say. "You'll see fish in there. Sometimes you'll even see a big bass." It's a big pond, four acres, with a good natural balance that keeps it clean. Dad had it cleaned out and stocked after they bought the place and the fishing is quite good. The kids want to take out the canoes, but again get turned down. Plenty of time for that tomorrow, they're told, as they are staying a few days before heading home.

As we head back up the slight hill towards the new house, my sister remarks, "Mom and Dad really found an awesome place when they found this old farm. We'd love to have something like this, but just that old farmhouse on a two acre lot would be like two million dollars in the Bay Area!"

"Yeah, Mark, this place really is remarkable," says my son-in-law. "So you and Rebecca are going to move out here?" Turning to Rebecca he asks, "Becca, you buyin' in to this plan? You weren't exactly raised a tomboy. Nearest nail salon gotta be twenty miles away!"

"Hey, smart ass! I'm gonna love it here," My wife retorts. "And I'll outfish you any day. Who do you think taught your wife how to bait a hook anyway? Besides, the hair salon in town does nails and she's quite good. So there!"

The kids head off to tell about their adventure to the other kids and we all rejoin the party.

The merriment and memories continue long into the evening. As guests begin to leave we all start making claims for our sleeping quarters. Between my parents' house and the old farm house there is room for all the adult children with a few grandkids sprawled out on couches or on the floor. We cherish the comfortable closeness, wondering if we will ever all be together there again.

Chapter 4   Gathering, September 11, 2018

My wife's building comes into view. I turn the corner heading up the drive to the large parking areas. People are everywhere, kind of like at the school, kind of looking like a fire drill, but less organized. An older model Mustang heads out past me with five people in it, three crammed in the tiny rear seat. It being such a nice day, someone must have decided to bring their classic car to work, lucky for him and his friends.

Again, the stares, and again, people moving out of my way. I am hoping I won't need to drive through the parking areas. They are full of people, many staring bewildered at their cars with the hoods up; a few people are actually trying some useless repairs.

Security people approach me as I pull up to the visitors parking area near the main entrance. I glance at the shotgun wrapped in the blanket, and rest my hand on the pistol grip of my Glock. Two gentlemen in security uniforms and a well-dressed woman come up to the open window of the van.

"Can I help you with something?" the older of the two guards asks.

"I'm looking for my wife, Rebecca Mays, she works in payroll," I state.

The woman says, "I know Becca Mays, she works here. I saw her a bit ago, she was in the rear parking area with some of her friends."

I don't want to have to circle the building. Over three hundred people work here. Confusion is starting to set in, and driving through all these parking lots and people is not a good idea. "Could you send someone to let her know her husband is here to pick her up?" I ask, as if today was just another normal day.

The woman says no problem, and finds a nearby subordinate to go seek my wife.

The younger guard steps a little closer and asks, "What's going on here? How come your van is running? Why won't anyone else's vehicle start? Nothing is working but you got a vehicle that runs."

At that moment I start to hear the low whumping sounds of helicopters in the distance. I look in the direction of the sound, coming from nearby Murtha Airport. As it grows louder I say, "Hey, look there. The National Guard is up and running as usual." We all turn and watch a flight of four helicopters come over the tree line. Two Apache attack helicopters flanking two Blackhawk transport gun-ships.

My mind races and I quickly realize the military is activating to evecuate the VIPs from the Shanksville, Flight 93 Memorial ceremony. An hour in, and hardened assets are being deployed. I don't recall who the VIP's are, but I am sure it's at least the Secretary of Homeland Security and a few Four Star Generals. The nearby military/civilian airport has to be in full operational mode. All hardened assets will be moving to protect the elite. I briefly wonder the fate of the average citizen, who has placed too much reliance on the government it thought would take care of them. Thousands of people in Shanksville will be left to their own devices as the elite are whisked away to Camp David or Greenbrier or some other hardened site.

The young guard says, "Hey, we got things coming back on line! Wonder if my cell phone is back up and workin' agin?" He fumbles for his connection to everything he thinks is real. I thank God for the short distraction.

The flight of helicopters overhead has distracted everyone. Even though it's only been an hour, everyone knows it's not like a normal power outage. Computers are shut down, cell phones may power up but have no bars. Some battery powered equipment works, but anything connected to the grid is down. Cars won't start. Plumes of smoke from distant fires can be seen, but there are no sirens wailing. All mechanical sounds are gone, no traffic, no horns, no twenty-first century background noise.

The young guard looks up from his inoperable cell phone. "Ain't workin'! I don't like this whole shit pile," he says as he looks around. "Ain't no cops or ambulances runnin'. I ain't heard nothing over the radio, and I see…Crap! I see at least four fires going up! This is bad, mister, this is bad. I heard 'bout shit like this, and this is bad!"

I start to feel something bad coming myself, but try to empathize with the young man. "I know what you mean, young man, I know this all ain't right. Can I offer you a word of advice, what I think?"

"What do you think old man?" he asks, irritated.

"Go home to your family. Sit with them, hug them, and pray to God for forgiveness and protection. What has just happened is an EMP, and life is going to get very hard." I struggle with the next words. I want to say "Pray with me now. The Lord will hear your prayers, the Lord will be with you," but I am not strong enough to say them.

"EMP! I been thinkin' that, old man. Seen it on some survivor pod-casts. It's why ain't nothing runnin', ain't nothing gonna run!"

I'm feeling this situation is going to go down hill as I see Rebecca come around the corner with several other people, casually walking toward me. At the sight of me and the van

Rebecca beams a smile at me and waves happily. I wave back, and beckon her to hurry. She picks up the pace, and beckons to her friends to do so as well.

The young guard steps right up to my window and says, "How come you got a vehicle that runs? We're gonna need this vehicle if it runs, and nothing else does. I gotta get home, we gotta get these people home!"

"Don't panic, calm down," I say to the young guard. As Rebecca runs up to the van, I jump out of the van pushing the young guard back just by opening the door. I hug my wife hard as I whisper in her ear "Becca, it's an EMP and it's bad. I watched planes go down. We talked about this. Pray, Jesus will give us peace."

"Janet!" she exclaims as she turns to the well dressed woman, "What's going on?" I can hear the concern in Becca's voice, but she is being genuine.

"All our systems are still down, and I guess so is everything else, as your husband was just telling us. I don't know though, I think it's just a glitch. They'll get everything back up soon. Our security has a handle on things," Janet continues. "But I don't see any sense in keeping everyone here. Let your people know they can go home, but we expect them here tomorrow. I gotta go check with IT, and see if they have any news."

The young guard, feeling more confident in himself after hearing Janet's approval, asks me where I'm heading to. I dismissively tell him I'm picking up my kids and heading home.

"We got three hundred people here that need a ride home, your van is the only thing I see running. Mister, we're going to need to use your van," States the young guard.

"Whoa, friend!" I exclaim. "Hold your horses! This is my van, and I got my own people to get home."

"But sir, you just stated this is an EMP attack, and that makes this a national emergency. In my position, I can impose Homeland Security initiatives, and claim your property for the general good and use of the State. I have people here who need transportation and you have the means of transportation. Step aside, sir. I proclaim your van as Property of the State in an emergency situation."

"I don't think so!" I say incredulously, "Your homeland security initiatives don't mean squat to me. You just blew through several constitutional amendments with your shiny little badge. You ain't takin' my van, my property! You got no right, and you ain't got the balls!"

"Listen, you redneck tea-bagger, I was told about folk like you," the guard responds angrily. "Rights didn't mean shit then and don't mean shit now. Our training from Homeland Security clearly stated that the president's directive was that we take control of the situation as we see necessary in an emergency. I see your van as necessary and this is an emergency! Step aside old man, I am procuring this van under just cause."

I see this spinning out of control. I pray for wisdom, Christ has already given me peace.

Turning to my beloved wife I say, "Becca, get in the van! Check the glove box, and under your seat. Tell your four friends to get in the back. We'll give them a ride as far as we can."

Turning back to the security guard, I loudy state "Young buck, our constitution trumps your presidential directive every time. Emergency or not, this is my property, and you have no right to it. Stand down!" This is not going well.

"You old fart! I'll rip through you like shit through a wet sack. Step aside!" he shouts as he raises his arms to charge me.

Before he takes two steps in my direction, he is staring down the business end of my 9mm. "Don't make me let this rip through your skull like lead through bone." I calmly but sternly state, fully ready to use deadly force to defend myself and my property from this punk. "You're nothing more than a car jacker with a badge! Step back."

The older guard steps up and the grabs the young guard. "Jimmy, what are you doing? He's right. You can't just claim his property. I watched that video too, but that's bullshit. You can't be some Gestapo type. He's just trying to take care of his own. Calm down."

"Yeah, calm down, Jimmy" I say. And at the Lord's urging I add. "I will gladly help those I can help, but I won't be forced to help those I can't." Keeping the Glock rigidly aimed at Jimmy, I climb back in the van.

With Rebecca and her friends in the van we head back down towards the main road. I'm glad to see Becca has her Glock locked and loaded, held steady, in a ready position. We turn north, away from her office complex.

Chapter 5   Getting Janie, September 11, 2018

"Rebecca!" I exclaim, "I'm so glad I got to you! Thank God! I gotta pull off and regroup, babe, my head is spinning." I pull off by an AYSO soccer field and get out of the van, putting my hands on my knees and taking a few deep breaths. Becca gets out and comes around the van. I stand up and we hug deeply.

"I'm here, baby, I'm here," she whispers in my ear. "If God is with us, who can stand against us?" she quotes to me. I feel strengthened. She steps back and gives me a very concerned look. "What the hell is going on! Explain!" Her penetrating green eyes, full of wisdom and hope, lock with my eyes.

"Becca, we've been attacked. Someone, the Russians, ISIS, I don't know, set off an EMP. Everything electronic has been fried. What we talked about has happened. We need to get everyone to the farm," I say hurriedly.

"EMP!" Rebecca exclaims. "We talked about a depression. We prepared for bad times, not end times! An EMP! Oh my God! Mark! Oh my God!" she begins to weep.

"Becca, Becca, Becca! I am with you and God is with us," I tell her. "We will be okay, but we have to move forward." We embrace tightly again for a few more moments.

I step back, breaking the comfort of the deepfelt hug. "Who are your friends we have with us and where do they live? I felt we couldn't leave them there, but what can we do now? How can we help them? Eeergh! This is not how it was supposed to happen!"

We get everyone out of the van and I open the hood to make it look like we are broke down too. There are several college students and other pedestrians walking our way, so I figure we should try to blend in.

One guy, Adam, a hunter and outdoorsman, lives about ten miles north of where we are parked. I let him know what's going on as best I can. I let him know we can get him to the interstate overpass and he will have to walk from there. He gets it, and agrees. I give him some water, it's all I can offer. He sees the ARs and asks about them. I assure him he can get home before it turns bad, but that he should do so as fast as he can. He should be home in a couple of hours.

Two of the girls with us live nearby, but they are close to being hysterical. They hear me telling Adam he has to walk home and that unhinges them. We repeatedly try to calm them down, assuring them that we will do our best to take care of them. We pray together and that calms them. We assure them again that we will get them home safely.

We load back into the van and together plan our next moves. One of the girls lives about two miles further from town than where we are now. We head in that direction first. Without incident, we get to her front door. Her husband and kids are not there. She pleads with us to help her get her husband and children. We are torn. We cannot do that. Becca puts her foot down. "Tina, we kept our word to you and got you home! Your kids' school is not far away. You go get them and walk them home. You need to step up and take care of yourself. Take the first step now, cause we can't take it for you. You can do this. You have to do this." With that we load up and head back towards town.

The next girl lives literally two blocks from my stepson and daughter-in-law's house. A few miles on the back roads and a mile on the four lane gets us there. The four lane is surprisingly clear, most cars having coasted to the side of the road. It seems that stranded drivers have started to walk, either looking for help or trying to get home. We drop her off at her front door.

Georgeann, our last passenger, lives on the other side of town. I try to convey to her that I can't get her there today. I tell her how things are different, stalled cars, no traffic lights, lots of people being confused and walking, and how people will want to take my van just because it's running.

She has two young kids, who should be coming home from school, and she needs to be home for them. The Lord inspires me. Since we took her into the van, we can help her, need to help her. I know He will be with us, that we can help her.

Inspired, I ask, "You live in the west end, right?"

"Yeah, just on the other side of the tracks from the supermarket," she responds.

"This may sound weird, Georgeann, but I am a Christian man. The good Lord would not have had us pick you up if we couldn't help you. So I believe the Lord is with us, and we can get you close to home. You have to have faith in the Lord that we can get this done, okay?"

She looks at me, and suddenly she brightens, something changed in her. "I do have faith Mark, I believe you, with God, we can do this."

I laugh, happily, the first time in hours. "Yes, exactly! Let's put a plan together."

I let everyone know we would go to our daughter-in law, Janie's house first. Becca would stay with her and help her get ready to go. Then I would take Georgann as far as I could.

Two minutes later we pull in to Janie and Zach's driveway, I honk upon our arrival. We go through the side gate and rap on the back door. A few moments later, Janie's perpetually optimistic smiling face appears at the door with her beautiful two year old in her arms. "Hey guys! Welcome! What are you doing here?" she exclaims enthusiastically.

I take a deep breath and look at Becca, beckoning her to begin the conversation, to burst the bubble. Rebecca wraps them both up in a big hug and says. "I love you both so much." Stepping back and turning to Janie she says, "Janie, we got to talk."

Seeing that I need to move things a little more quickly, I butt in. "Power's out, right?" a wide eyed nod from Janie, "Cell phone won't work, right?" another nod.

"Mark," Becca steps in. "I'll handle this. Janie, we've been attacked. ISIS, Russia, Chinese, we don't know who, but what Mark is trying to tell you is that everything electrical is down. Cars, computers, cell phones, all down. And not just down, it's off permanently. An EMP. Zach and you, and all of us have talked about this."

Janie's beaming smile and bright eyes are fading as Rebecca talks. Her tanned face turns pale, and she clutches harder to her child. She reaches behind her and grabs a kitchen chair to sit down. "Oh my God, Oh my God, Be with us Lord. Oh my God" She mumbles.

You can see in her eyes that her mind is starting to race and calculate the next steps. She is the mother of five children, an eternal optimist, a survivor by instinct; fiercely loyal to her family and husband. "How do you know? Are you sure? Power could come back on in twenty minutes. How do you know?" she asks emphatically, but logically.

I explain the planes falling from the sky, and everything else that I have seen. Rebecca explains what happened at her office, and all the events that have happened so far including the overzealous security guard, and all the idled cars.

"This is not happening, this is not happening!" Janie repeats. Rebecca reaches for her hand.

I clasp Janie's other hand. "Yes, it is, Janie, yes it is. Pray with us." I say. "Dear Lord, we do not know why this has happened, but we know we must move forward. We are here by your grace, and by your grace we will move on, and follow the path you have laid before us. Grant us wisdom, dear Lord, grant us peace, in Christ's name, Amen."

"Janie," I say, "We need to get to the Reserve Center for Zach, then we are going to pick up your kids at school. We're all going to the farmstead like we planned. I drove past the school about an hour ago. All the kids were on the lawns, like a fire drill. So your kids are okay."

Janie looks at me, some fire starting to burn in her eyes. "Son of a bitch! Those bastards in Washington, Those bastards! We all knew this was coming! Those bastards!" She exclaims. "Send my husband all over the world to stop this shit, and do they keep us safe here at home! Noooo! So now this shit sits at my front door! Why! Because our leaders were too afraid to call an extremist an extremist, while sending my husband off to fight them, but only if they get shot at first. Bullshit, bullshit, bullshit!"

Janie has already set the baby in the pack-n-play and has started packing things from around the kitchen, very methodically. She has pulled out a few cloth shopping bags and is loading them with what I can see are important items, especially from a mom's point of view.

"Janie," I say, "We have the van outside. We have to get you and Zach and the five kids in. That's going to leave the rear seat area available. Pack clothes and boots and any things that are dear to you. I don't know if we can be back any time soon. Pack as if we will never be back."

"Mark," Rebecca barks, "Don't get her all alarmed!"

"Honey," she says to Janie, "I'm here to help you, it will be okay."

"Okay, my ass!" Janie barks. "Those bastards!" She stops and starts to cry, "I have five children…. they just stopped the world, from what you say" sobbing, "what about my children…. oh God, what about my children…"

Rebecca turns to me, "Get Georgeann home. We'll be ready to go when you get back."

***

I return to the van. I tell Georgeann since the highway seemed pretty clear I can take her to town, but not through town. This will put her only about a mile from her home and her kids, she can walk from there. I explain that if I tried to take her through town there would be too many dead street lights with stalled cars, and the highway is divided by jersey barriers. If the highway is blocked by traffic, I can't turn around. I would be stuck there, unable to help Becca and my family. She understands.

Five miles into town and the highway is relatively clear. I pull off at the last exit, dodge around some cars stopped at the light and get ready to make the U-turn that will take me back to Janie's house.

"Georgeann," I say, "you have to walk from here, but it's not far. This has all just started, so most people will think it's just a power outage. You should be safe for now. Stop at your house and make sure everything is okay, then go directly to the school and get your kids."

"Mark, I'm scared. What you all been sayin' don't sit right. Things are going to get bad, aren't they?" she says.

"Things are going to get bad, yes, Georgeann. But the Lord told me I could help you, so I did. The Lord has a path for you, follow it. Find friends and neighbors you can trust, form a bond, work together, and pray." I pull out my wallet, "Here's a hundred dollars. After you get the kids, go to the supermarket and get rice, dried beans, pasta, salt and a couple bottles of bleach, too. When you get home, fill up your bathtub, and anything else that holds water, garbage cans, jugs. You need water, food and protection. Worry about that." I want to tell her, "For the next two weeks it's going to be horrible. Then for two months it's going to get worse. Make it through that and you'll be okay." But I don't have the heart to.

I let her out and finish the illegal U-turn to head back to Janie's. No honking horns as I swerve past stalled cars and a few pedestrians, but a few raised fists, and one fingered salutes.

***

I arrive back at Janie's about twenty-five minutes after I left. A couple of bikes and older model cars and trucks were on the highway. Other than that I have seen nothing moving by civilians. Apaches and Blackhawks are coming and going from Murtha Airport and one big military transport airplane has landed. The airport is way at the top of the hill, and everyone sees what comes in and goes out. The civilian class transport for the bigwigs at Flight 93 must be dead so they are bringing in hardened military aircraft to move them out, I suppose.

Back at Janie's things are moving briskly. I am sure my wife and Janie had a good cry and prayer, then got up and got moving. Katie, Janie's mom, is there, too. "Bring clothes, and any meds the kids need, we got food."

"On it!" is the response I get.

"Winter clothes, too."

"On it, start loading, old man," my wife responds.

"Janie, what about Johnie's asthma meds?"

"I got three months of inhalers and six months of pills. After that…" she stops and looks at me. I give her a hug.

"He is a strong kid, there are homeopathic things we can try," I console her.

"I know, I know," she says. "The clean air of the country will do him well too."

Looking at all the duffels and bins that have piled up, I get worried. They got two bikes and a bike trailer sitting right there in the garage.

"Janie, have you tried Zach or Rocco's bikes?" Rocco is Janie's dad, and a very solid guy, in many ways.

"No! Do you think they might work? Oh my God!"

"I've passed several on the road, give them a crank!" I exclaim.

Janie grabs the keys for both bikes and jumps on her dad's 2010 Goldwing. Looking at us, she turns the key … and nothing happens. "Crap," Katie exclaims.

"It must have some electronic ignition stuff in it," I say. "Try the old Sportster."

Janie hops on the Sportster her dad gave her when she turned eighteen, and turns the key….brrrrmb, brrrmmmmb brrrm brrrmb brrrmb! The old bike starts up and begins to purr.

"Awesome!" I exclaim. "We got another ride! Hook up the trailer to the van for the overflow stuff and we'll take the bike with us."

Katie mutters something under her breath, and all of a sudden I realize how self focused I have become, how selfish.

"Katie, forgive me. That was Rocco's bike. And you all will need it. You all need something that runs. I'm being so selfish, I'm just caught up in the moment. I'm so sorry."

"No," Katie says. "That was Janie's bike and now it's Zach's bike. Rocco will be home from the shop. He'll get something running, we'll be okay."

Rocco owns a salvage yard and auto repair business. As I think about that I realize he has several dozen older model cars and trucks, and just as many bikes sitting around. Katie is right, he is probably putting something on the road right now. He and I had talked about situations like this, and he offhandedly said he would have something running quicker than I could figure out that my stuff wasn't running!

"Mom, you say that like you are going to stay here," says Janie

"Honey, your dad will be home soon. He'll get the Goldwing runnin', too, I am sure, that's his baby. Mark and Becca are right though, you need to get the kids and head to their farm. I'm going to wait for your dad. We have to check on your sister as well. Don't worry dear, we'll be okay. We'll be out to the farm too, soon," Katie says with confidence and compassion.

"So Mark," Katie says to me pointedly, "don't you go worrying about me and Rocco. We can take care of ourselves. You get Janie and the kids out of here safely. If we need to, we'll be out. And use the bike and trailer for heaven's sake!"

I hook up the bike carrier to the van and we all start loading bins and duffels.

"Mark, we have to figure out what to do about Britt and Kenny," my wife says, as she places a bin of toiletries in the trailer. "I'm most worried about Britt. If she worked today, she is miles from home, and that pharmacy is going to be a bad place to be once it gets dark. Those druggies will be targeting her store, they'll figure this out soon enough. They're smart. They'll take the opportunity to raid that place, I know they will." The concern and anger in her voice is very apparent.

"You're right dear, she's in the middle of the main shopping district and in a pharmacy. When the looting does start, she's in the bull's eye." I look at the Sportster, but in my 56 years on this earth, I have never ridden anything bigger than a moped.... I look at my wife, who I am sure knows my thoughts.

"Janie, we need you to go check on Britt." Becca states, matter of factly.

Looking up from a bin she is repacking to hold more winter clothes, Janie says, "What?"

"We need you to take the bike and run over to Aid-Mart, find out if Britt is working today. That place will be ripe for looting soon, and if she is there, we have to get her home," I say. "We can finish up here, we need you to do this."

"Oh, hmm, what? Go get Britt? No! No! No!" She responds looking around at all that has been packed, thinking about all that needs packed.

Becca steps forward and hugs her. "Janie, we love you like our own daughter, but Britt may get stuck in a bad place, we need you to go help her. We have come to help you, we need you to do this. We need you to help her. Katie, Mark and I will finish up here. Janie, I can't let my daughter be caught up at that drug store, you have to help her out. You have to do this. If she's not there, you can come right back. You wont be gone but a few minutes."

Janie looks around and sees how we have come to help her. She realizes now is her time to help too. With determination she responds, "That place will get bad. We need to get her out of there. You're right, the druggies will be the first to start trouble. Um, okay, what's the plan?"

"If she worked today, she's at the Aid-Mart, by the supermarket on Scalp Avenue. Grab the bike and take the back roads as much as you can. Park as close to the store as possible, even on the sidewalk in front of the store if you have to. Make sure you lock up the bike. Is Zach's 9mm here?"

"Yeah, it's locked up in the gun safe, I was just going to start loading the guns into the back seat." Janie replies.

"Take the 9mm with you, with two extra clips. You shouldn't run into any traffic that you can't dodge around. And you shouldn't run into any trouble you can't talk your way out of. But don't let anyone take that bike. It's your only link to us, and Britt's only hope of getting home to Kenny and her kids."

Janie takes a deep breath, "Okay, not what I wanted to hear, but I get it. So, do I bring Britt back here?"

"That would be the easy solution, but we're not going to get easy solutions today. We may not get easy solutions ever again," I say sadly. "You'll need to take her home. Kenny and the kids will be worried sick if we take her with us and they don't know where she is. You'll have to take her home, to Roxbury. Do you know the route to take?"

"I'll go down Eisenhower, and up Franklin into Roxbury."

"That's exactly right, you'll skirt around town that way. Come back the same way, but take Krings Street and Belmont through Geistown. It should be quicker and you should be able to scoot around any traffic jams. Does that work for you?" I ask. She nods yes, I can tell she is processing it all through her head.

Rebecca comes out with the 9mm, spare clips and a shoulder holster. Janie straps it on and puts on her leather riding jacket. "Check to make sure you can draw that pistol, honey," Rebecca says. "Mark had me practice, and it can be a little funny depending on the jacket you're wearing."

Janie grimaces, and does a few practice draws. "I don't like this one bit!" she says. "I'm not Wyatt Earp." She takes a deep breath. "Is this happening? Lord be with me."

"The Lord will be with you, Janie," says Rebecca. "You can do this. We are family. We are here for you. We need you to be there for Britt and Kenny, too."

"Janie, while you are at the drug store, pick up anything you think will be helpful, especially for the kids. Stuff that will fit in the saddle bags, cold remedies, vitamins, Tylenol, Benedryl, whatever you think we may need. Here's three hundred dollars. Hopefully they will take cash. Honey, give her anything you got," I say to Becca.

I take a deep breath and turn to Rebecca. "Rebecca, what about your RA? Can she get you anything that will help? Your meds are going to run out. Maybe we can even get Britt to get a few things from behind the counter… but…. "

Rebecca stops me "No, Mark, that will have us looting the drug store before the druggies do. We have been blessed. God will lead us on the path we need to follow. That path is going to be hard, I know that, you know that, but let's not compromise our values. That's a path we cannot go down." Turning to Janie, she says, "Get Tylenol and Tylenol PM, the generic stuff is fine, Honey." Once again, as strong as I feel in my faith, my wife proves to be stronger. With her pure selflessness, she is my rock. But Rheumatoid Arthritis is a debilitating disease, and I worry mightily about her health in the days to come.

Turning to Janie I say, "Janie, you gotta get going. If Britt is not at the store, come straight back. If she is, take her home like we planned. Let her know we will pick up her and her family tomorrow, and they need to be ready to go. Follow the route we talked about. If you are not back in two hours we will come looking for you on that route. So stay on that route, got it?" She nods yes with a bit of attitude. She's ready to get this done so we can go get her husband and kids.

"As soon as you're back, we'll go to the reserve center and get Zach, then we'll go get your kids," I assure her. She nods, then heads out, peeling some tire as she turns onto the main road.

Chapter 6   Electricity, June, 2016

I stand staring, somewhat baffled, at the battery rack, wiring, and control panels for the solar system we just finished installing. "So Paul," I say, "how do we go about giving this system a test run?"

Paul responds, "Actually, we can't do a full test today. But we can see by the power meters that everything is working. Final hookup to the grid has to be done by the power company. They have to test the grid disconnect system to ensure you're not putting juice back onto the grid in case they have to fix the lines."

"Yeah, that would be bad, I get that."

Paul adds, "They also will certify the system and install their gizmos so they can reimburse you for any power you put back on the grid, for the power they have to buy from you."

"That part I like," I say. "I'll take advantage of that program. But the $3,000 subsidy for the solar system, I just can't do that, Paul. I might as well go around to thirty of my neighbors and put a gun to their head and tell them each to give me $100 so I can put in a solar system. It's not morally right. Yeah, sure it's a government program, but where do people think that money comes from?"

"You actually would need to put a gun to their kids' head, because it all adds to the debt that will fall on their kids' shoulders," Paul replies. "But I think you should take the money anyway, Mark. The whole system is going to collapse, so take advantage of the handout while you can."

"That's occurred to me, believe me. But I still hope we can turn this ship around. If we actually get a president that will roll back all these cumbersome rules and regulations; the stupid programs, like paying to install solar panels, or worse yet, paying millionaires to invest in windmills, maybe then we can get this economy rolling again."

"But forget that, dude," I continue. "What about this power plant! Let's give this thing a test drive. I'm pumped to see if this actually works. Walk me through it again."

My oldest brother, Paul, would be classified as a geek. He has an electrical engineering degree from Penn State as well as an MBA from Carnegie Mellon and a computer masters degree of some sort from MIT. It's all way over my head. But he is way cool, loves to fish and hunt and likes to build things. We have a summer place in Canada and it is completely off the grid due to the power plant he designed. So I have complete trust that what he has helped me install is going to work.

Paul starts off. "Okay, first you got six solar panels on the roof, their peak capacity is about 1400 watts. See here, on this display is how many watts you're generating. Right now you're generating 1260 watts. That charges your deep cycle batteries over there. When the batteries are fully charged the power will then flow into the AC/DC converter and then to the inverter. The inverter sends AC power to the house. If you are producing more energy than you are using, the inverter sends the juice back out on the grid.

"This display right here shows how much charge your batteries have. And this one shows how much power you are using. These displays are all hardwired to the remote display in the house, so you can see what's going on without coming down here."

"This is way cool, brother!" I say with excitement. "So we are generating 1200 watts right now, awesome! The whole place has LED lighting, including spots. They pull less than 10 watts each, I could run every light in the house. Okay, but what about my fridge and pump? They're the heavy power sinks, right?"

Paul laughs out loud. "I told you. You'll need to expand this system, probably triple it to run the pump and fridge. The fridge draws about 750 watts and the pump another 1000 watts. And when your pump starts up, it draws about 2000 watts or more. This is just a starter system, but you got all the basics you need to expand.

"Look, Mark, we all know you and Becca are working on making this place a safe haven, where we can all come if it all goes to hell. And you've done a hell of a lot of work to get there, but this system is only a starting point. Everything you have here, though, is expandable. Eve and I have been talking about it, and we are going to double your solar panels and your battery bank. Six more panels and twelve more batteries will be here in the next few weeks. You got everything in place, adding on is almost like building with Legos. We just add on."

"Whoa, brother! That's quite generous! Thanks! You know you all are welcome here if it goes bad. That's mainly why I keep upgrading the old farmhouse. To have room for you and Eve. John and Jan, too.

"But back to the power system. I knew that we couldn't run the fridge, kinda. But we got to have enough juice to run the fridge. We keep Becca's meds in there. No fridge is not an option. And that pump starting thing is scary, too. Do those twelve batteries have enough juice to handle that?"

"Right now it's iffy, but with what Eve and I will add, it will cover it. But you need to look at the gravity feed water system we talked about. A water tank in the hayloft will feed the new house and the farmhouse. That will really cut down on how often the pump kicks in. And better yet would be to put in a gas-powered pump to fill the tank. Then you would eliminate the pump from your electric power consumption completely."

50

"Yeah, but I need a structural engineer to check out the beams before I put an eight thousand pound water tank in the hayloft.

"Back to this power system, Paul. I already poured the foundation for the windmill I told you I want to put in. Heck, I'm surrounded by mega windmills, I should put in my own small wind system, right?"

"You get enough wind up here for sure, so that's a good plan," says Paul. "When the sun ain't shinin', the wind's blowin'. So yeah, this system can bring that in, too. It will get wired in here, same as the solar panels feed the batteries. No different than adding more solar panels.

"And before you bring it up, yes, your job-site generator can be plugged in, too. But there is no system to automatically turn on the generator if the batteries are low and your other sources are not generating. But you'll know if you need to fire up the generator, just by checking the displays in the kitchen. If you ever get around to installing a permanent backup generator we can look into an automatic start up system or as a minimum, a remote start up from the kitchen, like on the island up in Canada."

"This is all way too cool, Paul. Thanks for designing this, but I want to bring up one more thing."

"What's that?" replies Paul.

"What about making this whole little building a Faraday cage? The crazy bastard in North Korea just set off another nuke. And the Iranians have been testing low earth orbit missiles. They can send us back two hundred years if they pull off a low orbit EMP."

"I'm not totally buying in, I don't think they have the technology to pull that off yet," replies Paul.

"'Yet' is the operative word there," I reply. "Anyways, I could buy replacement parts for this system, and store them in the small Faraday cage. But it would probably be cheaper to just put a metal roof and siding on this building and ground it rather than buy the spares. What do you think?"

"That may work, Mark. Good idea, let me think about it," Paul responds.

"Hey, let's go up to the house and see what Rebecca and Eve have got going on. Eve said she had some recipes for making jams she found at her mom's house. And they were supposed to make BLT's. Just don't mention John or Samuel Adams, don't ask, it's a long story."

We head back to the house, happy with a good day's work behind us. Another step taken in making Mountainside our safe haven.

Chapter 7   Activated, September 11, 2018

After Janie heads off, burning tire, Katie and Rebecca take turns entertaining little Sara as I continue to pack bins and duffels and load the van and trailer. I find enough rope and bungie cords to strap down duffels to the roof of the van. I start on gathering sleeping bags, comforters, camping gear, anything I can find that we may need for the kids and their comfort.

Mostly it is quiet in this residential neighborhood. I have seen a few bikes, and older model cars and trucks go by, but nothing to be alarmed about. I am assuming most people still think this is a normal power outage and things will get back to normal.

Another military plane lands at Murtha Airport and a few helicopter flights come and go. While strapping down the last of the bins to the trailer I see a military plane taking off from the airport. It makes me curious and I scan the skies a little harder. "Do we have F16s up?" I say, more to myself than Katie or Rebecca. We must, I conclude, they wouldn't be sending the bigwigs out if we didn't. That is reassuring in a way, but oddly chilling as well. Good to know our military was actually hardened against the attack; chilling in that the elite are being taken care of while the people are powerless, literally.

I hear another truck rolling up the road, sounds like it has no exhaust. It turns onto our street and stops in the short driveway. My hand moves to the butt of my pistol, but I quickly relax as I see Rocco's big frame in the driver's seat. Becca and Katie have already come out of the house because of the noise.

"Rocco," Katie exclaims as she runs and gives him a loving hug. "I told them you would be here," she states, stepping back and beaming up at him with a huge smile. Rocco goes about six foot four inches and well over two hundred and fifty pounds. His daughter's infectious smile is a trait obviously handed down from dad. He is a biker guy through and through; who married the preacher's daughter, literally. His big heart always ends up in the right place, but sometimes the path may be a little long in getting there.

"What in the hell is going on in this town!" Rocco almost shouts. "Nothin' is workin'; lights are out, traffic is stopped everywhere, people are walking around, not knowing what to do. It's crazy land downtown! I seen at least five wrecks and no ambulances. Cops are on foot, not knowin' what to do. The convenience store on Haynes Street got its pumps on fire and there ain't no fire trucks nowhere. One cop stopped me and wanted my truck. I gunned it. To hell with him!" He takes a breath. "I am so glad to see you all! Where's Janie and the kids?"

We take a few minutes to fill him in on what we all have seen and what we are doing. His expression grows dim. "This ain't good. Ain't good at all. But the military is up and running, huh? Well, that's something. Maybe Zach knows what's going on."

"Janie should be back any minute, then we're headed to the reserve center. Maybe you and Katie should go with us."

"I think so, we need some answers. But if what you are telling me is right, we need to make some plans."

"Almost too late for plans now." I say. "We were going to take the kids and grandkids out to our farm. Rocco, you and Katie are welcome to come. It will be much safer there. We already asked Katie but she wanted to talk to you and see about your other daughter first."

"I ain't runnin' off to the hills just yet. Me and Katie will be just fine. We got food and we can protect ourselves just fine if you know what I mean. I don't call 911. Guess I can't now, huh?" he says with a chuckle. "What do you think, baby? We ain't runnin' nowhere's, are we?"

"Rocco, I will stay with you wherever that may be. I have for forty years, and I ain't changing now. But let's keep Mark and Becca's invitation in mind. If it does get bad, we could go out there."

"I ain't imposin' on no one like that. I take care of my own, always have, always will. Asides that, Mark here would have ta hear me cussin' now and then, and then he'd go to telling me not to." He looks at me laughing.

"Ya know we is all sinners, Rocco. Givin' up cussin' is an easy one. Lord wants us to be better people is all I'm sayin'." I reply. "And there won't be no imposing, big fella. Your mechanical skills will come in mighty handy, and we'd be glad to have ya'. On your time, that is."

Rocco looks at Kate. "We got to know our other daughter is okay. And I want to see how things shake down here. Hell, most folk ain't that bad, we probably be just fine here. Big stink over nothin' maybe. But we'll get out your way if we need to. And I'd feel good knowing Janie and the kids are safe out there with you all. A little time in the country will be good for the boys, and little Sara, too."

We all start talking about what we think has happened and what's going to happen, playing out scenarios and talking about how much food Rocco and Kate have. We let them know about the food here at Janie and Zach's and we start to pack it and load it in Rocco's salvaged truck.

A little over an hour after Janie left, we hear her coming back down the road and we all smile as she turns in the driveway. She pulls off her helmet and is displaying her perpetual smile. "All good" she exclaims. "I got Britt and took her home. Kenny was already there and they were getting ready to walk to the high school to get Larson and Grace."

"How are they?" Becca asks.

"Britt is shook up, she wouldn't leave with me on the bike, but her boss basically forced her to. And she was a little freaked out about walking to get the kids, kept insisting that Kenny fix the car. Kenny has a handle on it though. He said they would be ready tomorrow for you to get them, assuming the power hadn't come back on. I think he said that for Britt's sake more than anything. There's wrecks everywhere and some fires. No one is responding. He knows that it's all gone bad."

"What were the roads like?" I ask.

"People where starting to walk the roads up by the pharmacy and supermarket, but I scooted past them. It was all clear down to Britt's, 'cept for a few small wrecks and stalled traffic. I came back up Ohio Street, hoping to save some time, but a concrete truck plowed into a fuel truck. They where both down over the hill, and there's a big fire going. It's so dry, I think the whole hillside is going to burn. No one's there but a few people watching, no fire trucks, nothin'."

"You came back Ohio Street!?" I shout. Janie looks at me, smile gone because of my angry outburst. "I told you to take Eisenhower and Krings Street! Both ways! Ugh, sorry, sorry, let me calm down."

A bit more calmly, but with urgency I tell her, "You need to follow the route Janie. If something had happened to you, God, we may never have got to lookin' on Ohio Street for hours! You have to stick to the route."

"Mark!" Becca says sharply, "Don't be so harsh."

Rocco steps in, "No, no, no, Mark's right. Janie, you got to follow a route like that. If something were to happen, we need to be able to find you. Now come over here and give your daddy a hug!"

Hugging Rocco tightly, Janie exclaims. "Poppa! Mom said you would be here! I love you Poppa! Oh Pop, what's going on, is it like Mark says?"

"Sounds like you seen it for yourself, little girl. Yeah, it's kinda bad. Let's go get Zach and then pick up the kids. Mark tells me you all are goin' to the farm with him and Becca till this blows over. That's a good plan. You'll be safe there."

"What about you and Mom?"

"We'll stick around here for bit, little girl. We'll come out if things don't settle down. Don't worry about Poppa and your Momma. We'll be fine."

***

After a final few checks through the house, and a check of the load and trailer, we all pile into our two vehicles to make the short run to the reserve center. Janie follows on the bike. This will take us right down the airport road, past anything that may resemble normalcy.

The airport road has several National Guard, Army Reserve, and Air Force Reserve units on it, thanks to Representative Murtha and his pork projects. So a lot of equipment and buildings will have been hardened against a nuclear EMP. I pray that we don't run into problems, but I feel it is too early for them to have started any serious crackdown on civilian traffic.

Five minutes later our little caravan pulls up at the gate to Zach's Reserve Center where they repair military equipment coming back from overseas. The gate is closed, as usual, but there are armed soldiers manning the gate, not the normal civilian guards. A guard at the armed ready position blocks the gate as a sergeant approaches the van.

"Sorry sir, no admission to the base at this time. You need to turn your vehicles around and leave the premises. I suggest you return the way you came. The airport road is shut down to all civilian traffic until further notice," states the sergeant bluntly but with no menace.

"My son, Zach Mays, Sergeant Mays, works here." I say, "We have his wife with us and we need to talk to him, let him know she's okay."

"I am sorry sir, there has been a national security incident and this base is on high alert, no one enters and no one leaves. You have to turn around and leave. You are not permitted to be here," the sergeant says more firmly.

By this time, Janie, on the bike, has pulled up and takes off her helmet, letting her long blonde hair fall down. Flashing her brilliant smile, she says "Joey! Stop the hard ass crap. I need to see Zach, so don't give me no bullshit or I'll tell Carrie who you where makin' eyes with at the summer picnic."

"Janie! Damn you. Janie! Okay, no threats needed, me and Julie was just havin fun... Hardison," the sergeant yells over his shoulder. "Radio the motor pool, let Staff Sergeant Mays know his wife is at the front gate."

"Thanks, Joey," I say with a grin, "we'll turn around and get pulled off to the side, okay?'

"That would be good, sir, thank you," Joey responds.

After turning around, we wait a few minutes, not so patiently, but we have no choice. Janie had put on a good show for the gate sergeant, but we all can tell she is very nervous. "No one enters, no one leaves," remarks Rebecca, "That doesn't sound good. I need to be with Janie, be there for her, this may not go well. She won't want to leave without Zach." Rebecca gets out and walks over to talk with Janie. Katie joins them.

Another flight of helicopters comes in from the south, from Flight 93 Memorial, two Apaches and two Blackhawks again. They aren't playing games. They quickly take off, but this time they are heading east. Interesting, maybe all the bigwigs have been evacuated already. Thousands of civilians will be left to fend for themselves. That could be a problem.

Soon we see Zach coming towards the gate at a fast jog. I get out of the van and walk over to where Janie, Katie and Rebecca rejoice as Zach comes up to the fence. Janie has a smile bigger than usual upon seeing Zach. "Honey! What's going on? Mark say's we've been attacked. From what I've seen, he's right, and you're on lock down! Can't you come over here and give me a hug," she says pleadingly.

"Baby, baby, baby!" Zach empathizes. "We have not been locked down. In fact we've been activated. It just came down the line officially about thirty minutes ago. I am sooo sorry, baby," Zach says earnestly. "We knew this could happen, honey, we just never thought it would happen this fast."

"Oh my God, Oh my God, Oh my God." Janie is almost in tears, "What's happening, Zach? What going on?"

"Honey, we have been attacked," says Zach . "But I don't know much, the rumors are flying. They say nukes in DC and New York. They also say high altitude nukes. I don't know, it's chaos, babe. They are doing everything they can to scramble all the bigwigs out of Shanksville. We are trying to get any vehicle we can runnin'. But most of our vehicles are shot. I don't know what to tell you, babe, It's chaos and no one knows what's going on."

Looking at Zach, I state, "High altitude nuke definitely, Zach, EMP. I watched three planes nose dive. Everything electronic is shut down. We talked about this, Zach. North Koreans,,, Islamist extremists. Someone pulled it off, Zach. Some evil bastards have sent us back two hundred years." I look away, off to the distance, to hide my tears.

"Zach!" Janie almost yells, "What are we going to do? What do you mean we've been sent back two hundreds years? EMP! That was just you and Mark talking conspiracy theories, that was just you and Mark talking nonsense… Oh crap… it has happened…. Oh, my God."

We are interrupted by Specialist Hardison. "Sergeant Way! Your XO is looking for you. He wants you back in the motor pool. You need to wrap this up."

We have to move this along and it's going to be rough. I pray for wisdom and patience. "Zach, we are ready to take Janie and the kids out to the farm like we talked about if something like this happened. But you were supposed to be going with us." Through the fence, I look at him in the eye. "Zach, Janie and the kids need to be at the farm with your mom and me, it's going to get bad here. But it's your call. I can't force it." I walk away.

Zach, Janie, Katie and Rebecca stand together, but not together, a fence separates them, but God unites them. I can see them talking, arguing, crying, praying. I pray too. Janie and Zach may never see each other again. This is beyond my weak abilities of compassion. I have a good sense of what is right, but I am not good at compassion. I have to stand aside. God's will be done.

The sergeant named Joey walks over and tugs on Zach's elbow. Zach pulls away. Zach motions at the gate and says something pleadingly. Joey opens the gate and Zach and Janie hug tightly. Rebecca and Katie then hug Zach too. Janie and

Zach hug again and kiss passionately. Rebecca, Katie and Janie turn and head towards our small caravan. Zach watches longingly and then turns back towards the motor pool.

Rebecca gets in the van and looks at me, tears rolling down her cheeks. "It's okay," she says, "It's going to be okay. Let's go get the kids."

Chapter 8   The Kids, September 11, 2018

"What's going on, hon?" I ask. "What's the plan?"

"Don't worry, honey. Seriously, do you always need a plan? Janie is going with us. We are going to get the kids now. Rocco and Kate are heading back to their house. Janie is following us to the school. Is that enough of a plan for now? Let me regroup here, babe. That was tough, but we worked it out,,, just give me a few minutes to process it all."

I know when to shut up and not ask questions, this is one of those times. Rocco pulls out around me and makes a right, away from the airport and back towards their home. I pull out and follow him, and Janie follows behind me on the bike. We go all the way back past the kids' house to avoid the airport. Rocco and Kate pull off at their driveway. I look at Rebecca and she is staring straight ahead, lips moving in a silent prayer. I know to keep going, to get the kids, as she said. She will fill me in when she is ready.

I start taking a few back roads that will skirt the shopping plazas and office parks. There are people in front yards gathering and talking. There are some people walking, including mothers with baby strollers and children. I think people are starting to realize this is different, that they need to start taking action for themselves. They are starting to figure out that the school buses aren't going to be dropping off their kids. They aren't going to take the minivan for wrestling carpool today. The sooner they figure it out the better.

We still need to dodge stalled cars, especially at the few non-functioning traffic lights we need to pass. Those get hairy a couple of times, crowds of confused and angry people at a bottleneck. To get people to move out of the way, we need to do some maneuvering and horn honking, at speed a few times.

We have the advantage of speed and bulk. I will use that edge. And how is God judging me as I do this? My soul aches. "Take care of those you can take care of, if you are helpless, then you can't help others, your time will come," I hear in my head. Am I just justifying my actions? I don't know. I keep moving forward, Wife, kids, grandkids. But how does that square up with my priority of life guidelines: God, Family, Community, Self? Family above community? But am I putting family above God and what he wants me to do? I need to talk this out, but there is no time now. "Be with us, God," I pray.

***

We come out on the road my wife's office is on. The schools are on the same road. Janie gears down and speeds past me. Turning into the elementary school, it still looks like a fire drill, but a bit more chaotic. Parents are starting to show up to get their kids. Most are on foot, but some are not; a few bicycles, one old motor bike, an old truck, a few classic cars and a couple of quads have been put in service. Five hours in and people are starting to get resourceful.

We pull the van and trailer off to the side of the main entrance as Janie takes her bike right up to a few official-looking administrators. She pulls off her helmet and, I'm sure, beams her bright smile, asking about her two younger boys. There is some gesturing, some shaking of heads. Janie shows an ID. The officials nod but start pointing at her bike, with her countering and pointing at us and the van. Someone is sent off in the direction of where the kids are running and playing.

Finally the boys come running to her, smiling. They seem unaffected by the situation, still innocent, enjoying a long recess on a beautiful late summer day. Janie sweeps both of them up and hugs them tight. I cannot see, but I am sure she is crying tears of both joy and apprehension.

She grabs each boy by the hand and walks them over to us. She still has tears in her eyes. As she helps to load them in the van she smiles, keeping up a strong face in a difficult situation. "Three on board, two more to get. Let's keep moving," she says. "I'll lead us over there."

"Okay, Janie, but don't stop for anything," I respond.

A few turns and a half mile later we pull into the junior/senior high school. The same scene unfolds, except no kids running and playing, a little more somberness in the air. From this high on the hill, the plumes of smoke from several fires can be seen. Additionally, the lack of traffic and dead cell phones and laptops has let this older set of kids know the situation is not right.

Janie pulls up to what seems to be a check-in point, where other parents have gathered. She again shows her ID and after a brief conversation it seems as if the kids are going to be brought to her again.

With nowhere else to go, we pull into a nearby parking lot. It's a little too full for my liking and a few too many people are checking us out. We are not the only running vehicle around, but we are attracting too much attention. A large passenger van, fully loaded, with a loaded trailer, we stick out like a sore thumb. I worry about the glances we are getting from a few groups of people gathered around the other stalled cars.

I see a group of what must be parents, about ten people, with several teenagers in tow, looking at us and then start walking towards us. I don't like the vibe of the situation. They look angry. I hear one man shout, "Hey, your van is working?

Can you help us get our kids home? You could use that van to help us get our kids home."

I look around for a way out. Some honking and aggressive driving will probably clear a path, but we have to wait for Janie and the kids. I notice a "gun-free zone" sign and formulate a quick plan. I look at Rebecca, "I'm going to go talk with them. Get in the driver's seat. If this doesn't go well, just drive, do what you need to do to get you and the kids out of here. Don't let them take the van."

I pull off my jacket as I get out, making sure my Glock is clearly in view. Looking at the closest woman with two teenaged kids, I ask, "Where do ya need ta get to?"

"We live over on Oakridge. It's only about a mile away," she responds. "It won't take you long, and those three kids over there only live two doors down, so you could take us all in one trip."

"Ma'am," I respond politely with a smile, "when you were in high school, how far did you walk to catch the bus?" I am hoping for a good answer here.

"Well," she says a little taken off guard, "Umm, we got driven to school, we rarely walked."

Wrong answer, I think. "Lucky for you," I respond. "I got rides when I could, but we all usually walked to school, two miles. I don't mean to be rude, miss, but if you only live a mile away, you could be home in fifteen minutes. You walked here right? Why not walk home?"

Louder, I address the small but growing crowd. "Listen people, I would like to help you but I can't. I have my wife, and five grandchildren. I have to get all the way to Central City. We can't walk there, and this here van of mine is taking us there.

"You all live within a couple of miles from here," I continue. "The buses aren't running, they may not get running today. I suggest you quit thinking someone is going to come rescue you. Take matters into your own hands. You all can walk home. Enjoy the time with your kids and enjoy the beauty of this great earth God created for us."

"But sir," a woman from further away speaks up. "Things ain't right. Nothing's workin'. I saw some planes crash and we can see the fires around town. You seem to know what's going on. You got a van that's workin', and you're grabbin' your family and getting outta town! Tell us what's going on!" she almost yells at the end.

I feel compassion for these people. "Listen up, and I'll tell you all what I seen and heard. I talked to my son at one of the reserve centers, we been attacked. Probably knocked the grid out, internet too. Things are going to get bad, so again, I suggest you all get home. Hopefully they'll get this worked out soon. If you're a prayin' kind of person, I suggest you pray. If you're not the prayin' kind, I suggest you start."

"Attacked you say! I knew it!" says someone else. The crowd starts talking amongst themselves, some grumbling, some shouting at each other, at no one, at God.

The low rumble of Janie's Harley alerts me that she must be coming with the other two boys. The crowd is still too heavy for us to move the van through. I need to get them moving.

"Y'all gotta get movin', y'all gotta get your kids home. I can't help you," I state loudly over the crowd noise.

They all stare at me a little dumbfounded, then start to move off.

I maintain my position in front of the van, authoritatively. Janie idles the bike up to the van with Rusty and Blake trotting behind her. The boys load into the van. I motion for Janie to come over, which she does.

"This is a little sketchy, but I think I've sent them on their way. I'm going to jump back in the van and lead us out of here. I want you to follow us, but if you can help by being aggressive with the bike, I need you to do that. Can you do that?"

"A little people versus bike chicken game? Can do," she replies. "You got my kids, I got your back."

As I walk back to the van the small crowd has started to disperse and Rebecca scoots over to the passenger seat. I jump in the driver's seat and start forward with our little caravan.

Wife, yes. Kids, working on it. Grandkids, got five, four more to get. Okay God, maybe this will work out… But we still need to get back to the farm.

***

And here we are, one of the few vehicles running. I have my wife beside me, on edge, alert, processing the situation, but ready to be a grizzly momma if needed. Two year old Sarah is strapped into her child seat behind me. And four of my grandsons are buckled in and ready for the ride, almost acting as if this were a video game and not real life. Their momma is riding scout on a 1984 Harley. Not to mention the overloaded trailer and the duffels strapped to the roof. We need to get home before we attract too much attention.

The ride back to the farm goes relatively smoothly. We have to dodge the same wrecks and more people. Janie gets aggressive with the bike a few times and I lay on the horn to help move people out of the way when needed.

The coal truck accident that had started a fire is a bit scary. The fire has spread to several acres of forest. It being late summer, all the dry wood and debris is burning rapidly. There are a couple of people there on bicycles and quads, staring at the inferno, but there is nothing they can do. How long will that fire rage with no one able to stop it, I wonder. After seeing the wrecks and this inferno, the boys now realize this is real, it's not a video game. The mood in the van is very somber.

Passing through Central City I see Reverend Wysinger on the steps of his Baptist Church, talking with a few town residents and parishioners. This is not our church, but my company renovated their kitchen a few years ago, and the reverend and I are good friends.

I feel the need to stop, to talk, to pray. I do not feel the onset of mayhem here that I felt in Johnstown. Here I feel a sense of coming together. Or maybe I want to feel a sense of coming together. God works in mysterious ways. He is telling me to stop here. So I do.

"Honey, I'm going to pull over here," I say. "I want to talk with Reverend Wysinger."

"Yes, that's a good idea, Mark. We can all pray together," She says calmly. She grabs my arm firmly. "Mark, I didn't think this would happen, but it has, it's scary! I'm scared." She leans in so the kids can't hear, "Mark, I'm afraid, I'm afraid for us all. Some of those people we passed at those wrecks, they were dead! And it's just going to get worse, isn't it?" I look at her and nod grimly.

I step out of the van and the reverend smiles. There are tears on his cheeks. Janie pulls in behind us. She and Becca unload the kids.

The reverend wordlessly steps forward and we embrace.

I step back and look the reverend straight in the eye. "Reverend, the world just went to hell and we're still here? What's going on? We been attacked and life as we know it has changed. I truly prayed for the Rapture, especially for my kids. Now what? Start over?"

"God has not taken us, my son. Our duty here on earth is not over. Seeing you and your family gives me strength. The Lord has plans for us, friend. We have to find that path and follow it."

The reverend turns to Becca and embraces her. "Sister Rebecca. Stay strong, sister." He looks at Janie, trying to recall a name from the recesses of his mind. "Katie?" He asks.

"Katie is my mom, I'm Janie," she responds. Pointing to each child she adds, "And this is Rusty, Blake, Jimmy, Mark, and Sarah."

I ask the reverend if we can have some time alone, that I need to talk with him in private. He excuses himself from the small gathering and he, Rebecca and I walk into the narthex of his church.

"Reverend, I'd like us to pray together before I tell you what I know and we talk of what's going on." The reverend nods.

"Dear Lord, We pray for your mercy and your grace upon us and all who love you. Too many have turned from you. Too many wish evil upon their fellow man. Too many have decided that you do not exist. We pray for all those who have turned against you. We pray that a seed is planted in their hearts that they may come to know you and love you.

"Now man's desire for power has brought trouble to us all. We pray that you will give us strength to prevail against evil, wisdom to make righteous decisions in times of need, integrity that we may keep an honest heart, love that we will need when facing hate and, most importantly, Lord, let us keep the peace in our hearts that we know through your son, our Lord and Savior, Jesus Christ, Amen."

The reverend adds, "Dear Lord, we know that if you are with us no one can stand against us. We know that the same power that raised Christ from the dead is in us through the Holy Spirit. We know that through you all things are possible. We pray that we keep our faith in you, in all things and in all ways. In Christ's name we do pray, Amen."

I ask the reverend what he knows. He tells me of a parishioner, Sammy, who is a ham radio enthusiast, and apparently had a shielded radio. He had stopped by about an hour ago. He had heard that both New York and D.C. had been hit with nuclear blasts. He had also heard that the power outage is widespread, basically all of the country. He had heard the same from other countries, as well, and other cities being hit by nukes.

Sammy was so shaken up that he came to the church for solace. He didn't think the reverend would be there. He thought he had been left behind in the Rapture, too. But he wanted to go somewhere to pray, to find someone to talk to. The reverend had reassured him that he was at peace with the Lord. But smartly, he had sent Sammy home and told him to listen to the radio and write down anything of importance.

"Wow!" I say. "That's worse than I thought it would be. D.C. and New York nuked? My son said the same thing. That doesn't make sense. An EMP attack and ground level nukes?"

I proceed to tell the reverend what I have seen from the downed planes to the fires and accidents and people starting to get on edge already. Becca adds in about the guard wanting to take our van at her office and the same with the crowds at the school. Tearfully she tells the reverend about the accidents and the hurt and dead people we have already seen.

"Reverend, we have tough times ahead of us. How are we, as Christians, going to protect and save our own, while still extending a hand of love to those in need? If we have no electricity, no way to move food, get money…society is going to collapse. People are going to die and there will be nothing we can do to stop it."

"Let's hope, no, let's pray that it won't be that bad, Mark," the reverend responds.

"We are far removed from most of what's going to go bad," I state. "We need to try and band together. We have farmers so we have food. We can make it through this. And eventually we will be able to help others. Help others learn to take care of themselves. But desperate people will try and take what we have, that's what scares me. How do we stop them, how do we help them? Can we help them? I don't know, reverend. We need to keep in touch. And I want to hear what Sammy finds out on that ham radio."

We talk some more. I bring up the fact that there are several thousand people at the Flight 93 Memorial. He had heard the helicopters off in the distance, and I explain my theory about the elites being ferried out. The rest are stranded there. I think most will head towards Route 219. But some will head this way. Sometime tomorrow, several hundred stragglers, or more, will be coming through this small town. They will be hungry, thirsty and desperate. It would be good if the town was set up to take care of their needs and move them along. The reverend nods grimly, he hopes to meet with his deacons soon to start and plan a path forward, to help their parishioners, and now, to keep in mind the needs of those who may be stranded.

I let him know that I will stop in the next day before heading in to get Britt, Ken and the boys. I give him a few suggestions for getting prepared for hard times like gathering blankets, firewood, water containers and such, even at this late stage. He thanks me.

As we head out of the church we notice that the crowd has gotten a little bigger. Everyone is polite, but questions are flying. These people have the Lord in their heart, but life has changed and they know it. They are looking for answers wherever they can find them.

We load up the kids and start heading out of town. We pass the Dollar General and I quickly pull in. There are a few people there but it is not overly crowded. I still have over $2000 in cash on me. "You still open for cash business I suppose?" I ask the attendant as I enter with Becca at my side.

"Yes sir," the young attendant says. "I'm just keepin track of it all here in this ledger book I grabbed out of the office supplies aisle," he says with a smile.

"How many cartons of Marlboro do you have?"....I proceed to load up on cigarettes for me and Becca. That bad habit reeling up again. I buy him out of candy bars as well. I also buy him out of sugar and coffee. The smokes, sugar, coffee and candy bars we load in the van.

Realizing the selfishness of my acts, feeling that angel tugging at my heart, I proceed to buy all his bottled water and as much food as I can with the cash I have. I buy mostly canned and dried goods. This I have him set aside and tell him it will be picked up by people from the Baptist Church down the road.

I send Janie back on the bike to let Reverend Wysinger know to have all the food and water picked up by his parishioners. I tell her to let Reverend Wysinger know that these supplies could be used to help any passersby to refresh themselves so they can continue on the path to Johnstown, or wherever they may be headed. It's several pallets full of food and water. I hope he has the manpower to move it and the wisdom to distribute it justly.

Janie is back shortly. She tells us the reverend understands our mission and will carry it out as best he can. He gets what we are trying to do and is extremely grateful for our generosity, to both any travelers and the help that it will be to the town.

Once again we set out down the road to our safe haven, the farmstead. I say a silent prayer of gratitude to my mother and father for having the wisdom and foresight to buy the farm. I know they are smiling down at us from heaven as we gather to this safe haven that they provided us.

Other than the distant plumes of smoke and a few stalled cars and trucks, the final few miles of the trip are uneventful. I see Thad's tractor parked next to the barn, but no sign of him. At least he is home and safe. My neighbor's house looks empty as we turn past it onto the long driveway to the farm. We are greeted by the dogs. They are happy to see us and oblivious as to how the world has changed. They don't know it, but the world has changed for them, too.

Eight hours after I watched three planes nosedive from the sky, it is still a clear blue sky, darkening to the east. The redwinged blackbirds are still skirting along the edge of the meadow. The goldenrod is still brilliant in the evening sunshine. Two blue jays are cackling in an elderberry tree. My beef cows are grazing in the meadow. Two hawks gracefully circle high above. The world changed for us, but not for them.

Chapter 9   Bacon, Spring 2014

"Rebecca! Rebecca, come quick! We have piglets! We have piglets!" I shout out as the early morning sun creeps over the tree line. Running to the house I slip in the thick dew. "Baby doll, baby doll!" I holler as I race in the door. "Martha had her litter! We have nine baby pigs! They are all suckling! You have to come see!"

Seeing God's work is an awesome thing. We see it every day and don't even notice. A child's expectant look, the leaves of a tree blowing in the wind, the joy in the wrinkles of an elder's smile, the beauty of a song bird flitting through a bush. God's miracles are everywhere, sometimes we just have to take the time to enjoy them.

"No no no" my wife mumbles… "Huhm, piglets, Martha! Oh!" she starts to waken. "We have piglets! Are they all healthy!"

"I don't know! Do you mean do they have ten pig fingers and ten pig toes! I guess so, how many toes does a pig have! Come on, you have to see this, it is soooo awesome. Coffee's brewing, and God gave us a big huge beautiful day to enjoy."

Obviously, we are very excited about the piglets. It is the first non-fowl reproductive event on the farm. We've been here three years. Last year we raised two pigs for slaughter. It worked out okay after we relocated the pigpen further from the house. The relocation was a good thing in two ways. The further away from the house the less the smell, which was much worse than we thought it would be. And being further from the house made the pigs more like farm animals and less like pets. But we still named them, despite all our declarations against it; John and Samuel, Adams.

The farm raises meat, not pets. John and Samuel Adams bacon and ham made it to the skillet. We both had a little trouble with the first batch of bacon, well actually only the first bite. It was darn good. Anything you raise, catch, shoot or grow yourself always tastes better. It can be some work and can get a little dirty, but the satisfaction of doing it yourself makes it all good. But you have to get past that first "Jace" duck egg, or "Sam Adams" pork chop. The thing to remember is to not name your animals,,,, and all our animals have names!

***

It's been three years since Dad died and a lot has changed and a lot has stayed the same. We host the family holidays and parties. Rebecca has perfected Mom's raspberry jam, and we have added black raspberries as well, my wife's favorite. We also have figured out how to do applesauce. We planted a couple sour cherry trees, my insistence. I love cherry pie, cherry cobbler, cherry cheesecake... but they are not producing yet.

We have begun to talk about the farm as a refuge in times of trouble. Things are hectic in the world. North Korea has tested a nuclear bomb. Iran has test fired intercontinental missiles. The Arab spring is more like an Arab Islamic uprising.

Things in America aren't much better. The government says unemployment is down but more people aren't working than ever before. They say "There's no food lines," but forty million people are on food stamps. So instead of being in a food line, twenty-five-year-old men with tattoos and body piercings are buying chips and soda on their EBT card as they talk on their government paid cell phones. Work is punished, even looked down on; why work when the government will take care of you? Sucking at the government trough is praised. It is a system that can't last.

My two brothers from Pittsburgh, my stepson and son-in-law have all talked about this place as a refuge or safe place in some fashion, often at my urging. I want to plant that seed of thought. Rebecca and I have talked about it extensively. We both agree, that as we can, we need to make the farm our refuge. I am no prophet, but I see that things could go bad. And if they do, we want to be in a position where we can help people, not need help.

My wife works nine to five in a middle management position and I have a fairly successful construction company. Sometimes I work a sixty hour week, but my hours are flexible enough, that between the two of us we have had the time to start to turn my parents' retirement home back into a sustainable farm.

Our neighbor, Thad, leases eighty acres for corn and helps us out with the animals as needed. We rebuilt the chicken coop and have twelve laying hens. We have a flock of reproducing ducks, the meat is dark and succulent. We trimmed up the apple trees and planted cherry trees. Becca mastered fruit canning and I am trying to learn the vegetable end of things. My dad's garden has been put back in operation and sooner or later we will master canning tomatoes. As much as we try, it ain't as good as store bought. We cleaned up the root cellar in the old farmhouse and have put it back in use. It is amazing how long potatoes last in a cool dry place. With the help of my daughter-in-law, Britt, we have an awesome herb garden, and she helps us with drying and storing them.

It's all a bunch of little things, but it adds up. And there have been no major expenses so far. Just a lot of labor, but it is a labor of love. Being a new member of the Mennonite church, using the talents and gifts that God has blessed us with to take care of ourselves and others, it all just seems to make sense, the way it should be.

***

It's a workday and Rebecca has to get moving soon, but our first litter of pigs is way more important. She throws on some jeans and a sweatshirt and grabs a cup of coffee as we head out the door. Following her down the hill, I start humming Trace Adkins' "One Hot Mama" and sing outloud "Do ya wanna?"

She looks back, slightly blushing, and says, "Oh, now you start! You know I got to get to work. Keep that thought till later, ya big old boar!"

Coming up to the pig pen, I notice Rebecca doesn't cover her nose as usual, as she sees and hears all the little piglets with the sow. She goes to open the gate but I quickly grab it and say, "Hold up. Let's stand back. It looks to me as if they all are suckling. She's accepted them. You remember Uncle Ted's advice, let nature take its course."

"Oh Mark, they are so cute! Look at them, so tiny and so huggable! And Martha is just laying there letting them suckle! You're right, we should leave them alone. Let's just sit here and watch them for a bit." Which we do; watching the miracle of God replenishing the earth, while my wife and I name the nine piglets…

Chapter 10 First Night, September 11, 2018

We pass the front gate, the old farmhouse, then the old barn, and pull up to the new house. The kids all jump out before we can barely get the van doors open. Janie idles up alongside the van and drops the kickstand on the bike, letting it settle. The kids run to check the chickens and pigs and head down to the pond; off and running like kids should on a farm. That's good. They have seen and heard some bad stuff over the past few hours, and for them to act like regular kids is good to see.

After watching her kids run off to explore, Janie turns to us and lets her feelings out. Reaching to Becca for comfort, her big smile turns to a frown and the rosy cheeks turn pale. "Oh my God!" she sobs. "What the hell is going on! The world is on fire! I've seen it with my own eyes! I have five kids to raise! And where is my husband! The same stupid bastards that let this all happen lock him down! Those bastards! Those bastards!" Becca holds her for several minutes as she sobs. Whispering comforting thoughts to her, but mainly just holding her, letting her know she is loved.

"Becca, I have to see what's working and what's not," I say. "I blew out of here as soon as I knew what was going on. I don't even know if the water is working." We put a lot of work and money into this farm to make it a safe haven. I know the animals are still alive and the garden is still growing. But I need to check out the power system and the water supply.

I unlock the house and turn on the lightswitch, and the light comes on. Huh? They were dead eight hours ago. Maybe something in the circuitry needed to reboot? Maybe God worked a small miracle? Did Paul say something about a reboot delay? Huh? Well, okay, the powerhouse faraday cage worked, A few hundred dollars well spent. I step over to the remote power display panel. It is dead, circuits fried. I have a spare in the faraday cage, but that can wait.

I walk to the sink and turn on the faucet. Water pressure is normal, that's good. I hear Becca and Janie enter behind me. "We have water and lights, stove should work fine, too. Why don't you all make some tea and start some dinner? I'm going to go down to the power house and look things over down there. Our display up here is fried so I don't know if we are generating electricity or how charged the batteries are."

They silently nod approval, knowing that some normalcy like tea and dinner will be good for us all. I remind them to be quick to the fridge, as it is a power drain, and to be spare on using the lights. There is plenty of daylight left, we need to get used to using sunlight instead of electric light.

I am being robotic at this time, moving on what I know needs to be done, not on what I want to do. I want to break down and cry, hug and be hugged, like Becca and Janie; but things need to be done. I have to keep moving. Time to process this all will come later.

I head down to the power house, glancing over at the kids. The younger ones are chasing the chickens. Rusty and Blake talk together.

"Hey, Rusty," I holler, "How 'bout you and Blake feed those chickens and then meet me down at the barn door and we can feed the cows?"

"Okay, Pap," They respond. Kids are much better off when they have something to do. They'll probably put out too much feed, but at least they have something responsible to take care of.

I step into the power house, which is supposed to be a faraday cage. The power is on so I know it worked, but I am still apprehensive. A look at the display panel raises my spirits immensely, all the displays are working! Power generation is only at 1000 watts, not unexpected at this time of day and with very little wind. Battery capacity is full and dropping slowly, again expected. Another display indicates we shut off from the grid, as the system should have. "Hallelujah! Thank you, Lord. Thank you, Paul!" I exclaim out loud.

That makes me think of Paul, and my three sisters and my other brother.

***

My oldest sister, Cathy, and her lawyer husband, Tom, live outside of Raleigh NC. He is a prepper and belongs to a rural militia. He is the one who first instilled the thought that we, as Christians, need to be prepared. "If we are desperate ourselves, then how can we help others? Christians need to be prepared, in a position to help," I remember him saying many years ago, when first talking about the farm being a safe haven. I pray that their preparations have worked out. They have four children spread across the South. I pray for them as well.

My youngest sister, Lessa, lives outside of San Francisco. Millions of people crammed on top of each other, many reliant on modern technology. Not just for their jobs but, more importantly, to have food on the shelves of the nearby super stores. She is pretty close to the city. I have no idea if she has any plans for an event like this. She is very resourceful, but I realize I may never hear from her again.

"Lorrie!" I almost shout out loud. She and her husband, Daniel, have a summer home near the ski resorts only twenty miles away. What are the chances that they are there for a holiday? If not, then she and my two brothers are in Pittsburgh, sixty miles away. We all said we would come here if an event like this happened. But it's a lot easier to say it than to do it. And we never really had a "plan," just a general idea or goal.

I say a prayer again, for all of my family as well as all of humanity. Sixty miles. Chaos will start in a couple of days, tonight in some areas. It could take them a week or more to get here. I pray they make it.

***

The cackling of the chickens over the new thrown food breaks me away from my thoughts of brothers and sisters. I have to go meet the boys to feed the cows. They are going to have questions. I hope I have the answers.

I round the corner to the lower barn gate and see Rusty and Blake standing together talking. Rusty, a big kid at sixteen, looks at me and says, "Pap, it's just me, you and Blake, the young ones ain't around and Mom and Grammy are in the house. We know something bad is going on, so lay it to us straight. Don't treat us like kids. Tell us what's going on."

I kook at him and Blake with pride at their directness and desire to be handled as adults. But I am saddened at how quickly they are going to have adulthood thrown at them.

"Rusty, Blake, come over here and sit down." I indicate some hay bales for us to sit on. "We been attacked, guys. America has been attacked. I don't know everything, but here's what I do know." I explain to them all I can. I tell them life just got different, that feeding chickens and cows would replace Game Boys and Game Boxes. That they may not see their friends again. That things may get hard, even violent.

There are a lot of questions, some very adult questions, some very childish, but they are still children, who are going to have to grow up very fast. They ask about their dad and I explain the activation. They ask about Katie and Rocco and I tell them they said they will be coming. They cry some. But in the end, they stiffen their backs and tell me. "Pap, we'll do everything we can! You'll see, we can help out!" I turn my head to hide my tears, tears of joy, tears of sorrow, tears of pride.

"Okay guys, we got four beef cows out there, and they're hungry. Let's go feed them!" They go charging out into the field, almost like a football huddle breaking up. But then they realize they have nothing to feed them with, they are running around fired up with empty hands!

"Come back here, you knuckleheads!" I shout. "You've helped me do this before. Rusty, get two buckets of food grain and put it in the feed trough, spread it out like I showed you before. Blake, take a whole bale of hay and spread it out around the feed area. They'll start on that once the feed grain is gone. We're going to count on you guys to do this, so pay attention."

The kids come running back and grab the hay and feed buckets, a little embarrassed but laughing at themselves as well. The beef cows mosey over, knowing food is being set out for them, a few low moos are let out as they approach. The sun is setting and a golden red hue is starting to display across the sky. No contrails to be seen. A deep blue sky settling to darkness in the east. Vivid reds, oranges, purples and pinks to the west. Two dark and ominous clouds of smoke, one to the east and one to the north. God created a beautiful world for us to live on; Man has managed to screw it up.

I send Rusty to gather up the two youngest children at the chicken coop and we all head back to the house. I see a soft glow of lights and again thank God for our safe haven. How many people across the country are facing darkness? Some may have candles and emergency flashlights. But most of America is surrounded by darkness, wondering what will happen, when will the lights come back on?

***

What about the big cities? A power outage like no one has ever seen. Many people will be holding each other, many babies will be conceived. But many will be taking advantage of the situation. The rioting, pillaging and plundering will be starting as total darkness sets in across the nation. The cops will be helpless to respond, the fire departments and ambulances will be grounded as well. It will be a society without rules to guide it. Without a moral compass, anarchy will reign. The only hope is the grounding force of God. But God and his morality has been scoffed at and ridiculed in this country, driven far away; removed from the schools, from the public square, from the courthouse, from normal conversation. A country without God is a godless country....

***

I think further of the far-reaching effects of a massive power outage; a massive EMP. Hospitals and nursing homes are a death field. Advanced medical equipment has stopped. Surgical rooms are darkened. Our great pharmaceutical industry has ground to a halt.

ATMs are dead. All electronic money, most of the money in the world, has disappeared into the Ethernet. Ownership of vast wealth is gone. The wealthy have nothing more than the property they sit on, their vast holdings erased. And what they sit on is threatened by mob rule. As I approach the front door, the kids running up to me shakes me from these morbid thoughts. The two youngest grab my hands as we enter the house. "Pappy, Pappy, the piglets are getting big! And you got eggs. We didn't touch them, we know we're supposed to get them in the morning. Can we get them in the morning! We'll be real gentle. Can we, can we?"

The innocence of the kids makes me smile. It's funny how God provides what you need in many ways. "Can you? All by yourselves?"

A chorus of "We can do it, Pappy. We can do it. Grammy showed us how, we can do it."

"Okay, okay. That would be great, you all can get us eggs for breakfast. Now let's go in and see what your Momma and Grammy have for dinner for us."

The mood in the house is somber. I am sure Becca and Janie have been discussing things similar to the thoughts I have been having. And Zach, being activated, has to have Janie torn up, She will put on a good face for the kids, but she is missing him dearly already, I know.

The ladies have made burgers and cheesy macaroni from what was in the fridge and on the shelves for dinner. We try to keep a normal conversation up during dinner for the kids' sake. But it is stilted. All the adults, and Rusty and Blake, are preoccupied with other thoughts. But they go unspoken.

After dinner, as it is already late, Janie puts the two young ones to bed and sends Rusty and Blake up to the loft to start putting away their clothes, telling them that they will be staying here for a while.

I pour Becca a glass of wine and grab a cold beer from the fridge. Silently, we walk out onto the porch. We sit together on the old porch swing, watching the darkness settle over our mountain retreat. I hold her tight and tell her I love her. She tells me she loves me, too. We sit silently together.

"Why are we still here, Mark?" Becca asks quietly, tearfully. "If it's as bad as you say it is, why are we still here? Why would God put us through this?"

"I don't know, baby doll. I don't know. When I saw the planes fall from the sky, I thought I would be taken up to see the Lord. I thought we all would be taken up. I prayed that you and the kids would be taken up. But we're still here. We're still here, baby doll."

She snuggles tightly, more tightly than normal. "Tell me it's going to be all right."

I sit silently for a bit, "I can't tell you that, baby doll. You saw what happened at your office, at the school, everything on the way home. Honey, it's going to be bad."

She moves away a bit but we still hold hands. "Where's God? Where's God, Mark? People are going to die, people are dying right now! Where's God?"

I start to cry. I want to reassure my wife. But how do I do that when I don't know either? I tell her. "I don't know Becca, I don't know…."

I look around as we sit silently together. The light dimly shines through the kitchen window. A couple of bull cows moan and moo at each other, the pigs grunt and snort as they do. The few clouds in the sky part, to let the moonlight dance over our fruit trees, garden and meadows. And I feel great comfort, God is here!

I stand up abruptly as the moon shines on what God has blessed us with and say, no shout. "Look Becca, God is right here! He is lighting the path! Look! It is all right here!"

"Stand up, baby doll! Look, even in the darkness God is showing us the path he has provided for us. It may be dark everywhere else, but there is light here. God is with us, who can stand against us! Hallelujah, praise the Lord!" I shout and do a silly dance on the porch, my wife looking at me like I'm a bit crazy.

She looks at me again hopefully, then she looks at the scene being illuminated before her. The fruit trees, the garden, the big pond, the meadow with the cows and the pigs and how it is all being lit up briefly by the moon. "Oh my God, Mark!, Oh my God, he is with us, he is right here with us!" The clouds close in again, as they do on a brisk September night. But it was enough for me, and it was enough for Becca. We both saw the light. God is here. He has provided for us. We doubted in the face of difficulty, but He has been with us for years, getting us ready for this moment.

Now we both know: we must use what He has blessed us with in a way that He would find righteous and just, with kindness and love. This will be a fine line to walk.

Becca and I pray together, we pray for wisdom, patience, love and compassion. We pray for our family and extended family. We pray for our country. I silently thank God for my wife, and her compassion. I know it will be a balance for me.

Becca and I sit on the porch for a long while, looking over the farmstead. She sips her wine, I enjoy another beer. We both enjoy a cigarette.

"You know, hon, we're going to have to finally quit," Becca says.

"Yep," I reply.

"Is that going to be a problem?" she asks.

"Yep," I say again. "But we got bigger things to worry about, so I have to let it go."

"You're worried about my meds, aren't you?"

"Yep." I say forlornly.

My wife has rheumatoid arthritis. It's not like your regular arthritis where your joints wear down with age. RA is an autoimmune disease; for some reason, your own body starts to attack the cartilage and membranes between your joints. It is very debilitating and painful if not controlled. Thanks to modern medicine, my wife's RA has been in remission. Those pharmaceutical companies are shut down now....

Rebecca responds, "I'm worried, too. I still can't process that. I don't want to go back to that pain. It's been twenty years with no pain, other than flare-ups. You have no idea babe, you have no idea of the constant pain..."

"I know, babe. I don't know the pain, but I know how it affects you. And I know how you bear down and work through it. We have a six-month supply of the biologics. And maybe a year's worth of the rest of your meds. We are going to have to go homeopathic after that."

"Wine and whiskey, huh?"

"And teas and ointments and rubs. Maybe we can try out a rub tonight? Along with some candlelight?" I say sultrily.

"The world just tumbled down around us and you want to go and get all flirty with me?"

"Go forth and multiply, sayeth the Lord," I say enthusiastically.

"It's a little too late to start multiplying now, old man!"

"Tell that to Sarah and Abraham," I say as we gently hold hands and head into the house.

Chapter 11 Second Morning, Farmstead, September 12, 2018

I sleep surprisingly well the first night of the new world. The love of my wife and the love from God, as always, keeps my heart at peace. I know bad things have happened in the world, and things are going to get even worse. This causes me to wake a good hour before my normal internal alarm clock would have awakened me.

It is before 5:00 AM, and as my mind kicks in gear, very quickly the situation at hand begins to overcome me. Mobs of hungry people may soon be coming through Central City. My step-daughter, her husband and kids are still in Johnstown. America has been attacked and we are at war, but with who? Thousands, no millions, of people are going to soon go hungry and die, mobs of desperate people from the city will start migrating to the country in search of food.

"Dear Lord," I begin to pray once again. "Thank you for the blessings you have granted me and my family. Grant me wisdom, patience, morality, righteousness and peace. May I follow the path that you have laid before me and may your glory, Lord, prevail in all things. Touch the hearts of those in need, dear Lord, and change the hearts of those who do not know you, who wish evil upon their fellow man."

I continue my silent prayer for several more minutes as I start a pot of coffee in the percolator pot, not the drip machine. Might as well toss that drip machine out, I think to myself. My prayer ends and a conversation begins. I ask questions, sometimes I get answers. Yes, I talk to God, and yes he does answer. Some may call it thinking out loud, or talking to themselves, or working things out in their head. I think of it as talking to God. He created us, he created our souls, who do you think that inner voice is that guides you?

The overwhelming answer is all big problems are a series of small problems. Tackle the small things, one step at a time. Take care of family first, which means take care of the farm, too.

I wake Becca with a cup of fresh hot coffee. She smiles and kisses me warmly. I let her know of my plans for the day. We need to get the normal farm chores done. She needs to feed the kids, and get them settled. We need to finish unloading the van and trailer, but that will entail deciding if the kids are staying in the new house or at the old farmhouse. With the idea that Britt, Kenny and the boys are coming too, I suggest they all move into the larger farmhouse.

But the most important mission of the day is to get Britt, Kenny and the boys. They are in Johnstown. The normal way to go to their part of town would be west on Route 30 then north on 219 towards town. That is right past the Flight 93 Memorial, where thousands of people are now hungry, tired, thirsty and confused. Some will be getting desperate and angry by now, as well. We both agree, I need to avoid those crowds.

I also want to swing through Central City and talk with Reverend Wysinger. I am hoping he has laid plans for moving stragglers through town. It bothers my conscience, but we can only do so much. Feeding them and sending them along is the best I can think to do right now. Maybe we can set up some sort of work for food and a security program for those who want to stay or have nowhere to go. Too much to think through. Again I silently ask the Lord for wisdom.

Becca and I move to the front porch. We have a beautiful view to the east, over the mountains, and the sunrise is spectacular. It is hard to comprehend that America has been attacked. I know that looting and killing and riots have already started, but here, it is so calm and peaceful. As the sun rises over the horizon, reality sets in. Two obviously large fires are burning on the other side of the ridge, the large plumes of smoke had contributed to the brilliance of the sunrise. Another large fire to the north is probably from the coal truck accident we passed the day before. Because of the westerly winds, these fires won't threaten the farm, but they bring us back to the reality of the present situation.

Becca and I decide that the kids should all move into the old farmhouse. Becca and Janie will oversee that operation. I will take the van with the trailer to get Britt and her family. First I'll stop by the church and see how things are shaping up there. I hope to recruit someone to ride shotgun with me into town. Becca, Janie, Rusty and Blake are to keep a watch on the front drive and not let anyone in that we don't know.

We rustle up the kids for breakfast and send the two young boys out to get fresh eggs. We all have scrambled eggs and bacon with toast; the toast is soon to be a luxury.

After unloading the van and trailer I sit down on the front porch of the farmhouse with Becca, Janie, Rusty and Blake. "Guys, things are a bit different than they were a few days ago. America has been attacked and it has shut down our electrical system. It's early yet, but since we have a farm, small as it is, people may want to take our food. We can't let people take what we have, otherwise we will go hungry. So we are going to set up a guard system, okay?

"Rusty and Blake, you both know how to shoot the 12 gauge pump and the 30/30. I want one of you on the front porch of the farmhouse all day, with the shotgun at your side. You can see the lane real good from here. If anyone comes down that lane that you don't know, you ring this big old school bell real loud and then you tell them to stop. You let them know you got a gun. Tell them we don't want no strangers comin' on our land.

"Becca and Janie, you both keep your side arms on you all the times, and I'm going to put the 30/30 and one AR 15 in the living room of the farmhouse. If you hear that bell ring, you come in the back door and come out the front door loaded to stop anyone on the road.

"Anyone looking for help, send them on to the church in town. Tell them that there is water and food there. If needed, give them a couple of our throw away bottles of water. But do not let them past the fence line. No need letting people we don't know see what we have back here."

"So Pap, what do we do if someone comes down the lane?" asks Blake.

"Ya tell em to stop and ya ring the bell, you knucklehead. Ain't that what I just said?"

"What if they try to come on our property, if they don't stop?" asks Rusty.

"Fire a shot in the air and then point the barrel at them. By that time your mom or Grammy will be here. But if you feel threatened, if they point a gun at you, then don't hesitate, shoot 'em."

"Whoa, really, like in Mortal Combat?"

"No, not like in Mortal Combat. In Mortal Combat no one gets hurt, no one dies. This is real, guys. I don't think anything like that will happen. But I want you to be ready if it does."

I look at Rebecca and Janie. They are a bit ashen faced. "This is real, ladies. Stay close and be prepared. I don't think it will happen today, but we need to be ready, to be thinking about it. Someday, someone bad will come down that lane wanting our stuff. We have to be ready when that happens."

Becca turns away sharply and heads back into the house. Janie stares at me sternly and nods her head. Becca is pissed that she has to do this, but she knows that she does. Janie is being a momma grizzly.

    Before I leave, I go in and hug my wife and tell her I love her, and she responds in kind. We have done that for twenty years and we are not going to stop now. I jump in the van and head out the lane. I see the boys sitting on the front porch in the rearview mirror.

Chapter 12   Second Morning, Central City, September 12, 2018

I pass the house on the corner before hitting the paved road. No activity. I hope they make it home from wherever they are. Further down the road I pass Thad's house. I can tell they are home and active. Good, he is a good man, they are a good family. I keep heading towards Central City, still swerving past the same stalled cars as yesterday.

I enter Central City through a back road. I see a lot of people out walking and pass several old farm trucks going this way and that, many loaded with people and supplies. There are a few quads, bikes and bicycles moving about. People can be resourceful in finding means of transportation.

Before I turn onto the main road that will take me out of Central City and onto the state route towards Windber and Johnstown, I encounter a makeshift road block, two cars and a picnic table with a couple of guys armed with hunting rifles. The church is just up ahead. I can see a few dozen people already lined up there, many obviously out-of-towners heading away from the Flight 93 Memorial.

I recognize one of the guys at the roadblock as I pull up. "Hey Jimmy, I see you all are trying to get organized here. What's going on?" I ask.

"Hey Mark, good to see you," he responds. "It's gone to shit, Mark. No power nowhere. I hear we been attacked, nukes. Freakin' Iranians, maybe the Russians, too! I hear the whole freakin' world has been hit. They say when we got nuked, we nuked everyone else. Dude, this is freaking end times shit. Now we got these city folk from the Shanksville Memorial starting to move through here. Chief Wills said we need to move them to the church for food and water and then to move them along. Says we need to try and protect our own while moving these city folk along. It's nuts, man! What do you know? I hear you supplied the church to help out these city folk."

"I ain't sure about all that nuclear war shit, but maybe you ain't wrong," I respond. "We definitely got attacked, and it was definitely nukes, but probably high altitude nukes, no radiation, but it kills all the power grid. Old trucks and stuff will work, but nothing with computer parts. So you all are organized to move the city folk towards Windber and Johnstown?"

"Yep, but most of these people are from New York, Baltimore, D.C. They keep askin' for the FEMA representative or our National Security representative. I tell them we ain't got that and send them to the church. It's only been a few people so far, but they're feisty!"

"Keep sending them to the church. It's the only place they will find nourishment, in more ways than one!" Jimmy laughs along with me at the truthful pun.

"I see you're armed, stay alert for bad asses. If someone threatens you, defend yourself. We can't let people think we're pansies. As you said, we were attacked, You are now our homeland security. I ain't relying on FEMA, I'm relying on you, you got that, brother?"

"You can rely on us, Mark," Jimmy and his friends respond. "I don't want no FEMA shit around here anyway. We can take care of our own."

This roadblock is in the wrong place, I think. But at least they are implementing some kind of control, some kind of authority. Better plans need to be worked out. I don't think we'll see armed bandits on the second day, but they will be coming.

94

The guys move the table out of the way and I proceed down Main Street to the church where a couple of dozen people are resting, eating and drinking bottled water. Another dozen or more are heading towards the church. By their dress and demeanor, I can tell they are refugees from the Flight 93 ceremony. I pull into the church's parking lot and several people approach asking if I am part of FEMA and if I can give them a ride. I hide a laugh as I tell them that FEMA left them behind when the last chopper left Shanksville. I let them know I will help them, if I can, but that I'm here to talk with the reverend.

A well dressed man, a bit out of shape, demands of me that I take him and his family to the Murtha Airport, that as an American citizen, I owe him that. I look at him and see he has a plate of mac and cheese in one hand and two bottles of water in the other. What I assume to be his wife and slightly overweight kids are similarly well supplied from the church.

"Sir, my name is Mark Mays, and I'd be glad to help you out. But I have to ask you where you got the food and water?"

A bit confused at the question, he responds "Why this church here must have been a FEMA depot and they were ready for us. You know, the Flight 93 Memorial is just a few miles away, so FEMA had it set up."

"Well, let me set you straight on that, my friend. Your help came from this church, not FEMA. The food and water you are eating and drinking came from this community not from the federal government. You have asked for help and we have helped you. I suggest that you quit relying on the government to help you and that you rely on yourself and your faith, if you have any. Be grateful for what you have, and think twice before you demand more. Murtha Airport is about twenty miles north. I suggest if you start walking now, you can be there by nightfall. But don't expect no airlift out, the airport is pretty much shut down, too."

The well-dressed man looks at me indignantly and responds, "What! You expect us to walk twenty miles! You have to help us!"

"You have food on your plate and water to travel with. That's more than you got from your esteemed FEMA at Shanksville, isn't it? But I'll see if some of these farm boys will start a relay system to get you closer, sir. Do you have anything to offer in return for the ride?"

"Offer something in return for a ride? I'm the Second Under Secretary of State for Environmental Protection liaisoned to the Department of Defense! You people work for me! I demand a ride to Murtha Airport!"

"Sir, the office of the second under secretary of state for environmental whatever doesn't exist any more. In fact, you and your regulations probably put a lot of these men out of work. A lot of the men driving the old trucks that could get you closer to Johnstown, they're former loggers and coal miners. I suggest you keep your former occupation quiet."

"This is nonsense! I demand to see the FEMA representative! I deserve respect!"

"Sir, a silly ass title deserves nothing. Your FEMA representative probably got the hell out of Dodge on the last airlift out of Shanksville. I suggest you start thinking about respecting the people who are helping you. I wish you well, sir. I have more important things at hand. I have to move on." I turn and walk away as he sputters indignantly.

***

I am not going to leave my van and trailer in this parking lot with this crowd, especially after dressing down mister high falutin and his hefty family. Our little commotion with mister fancy pants must have been heard by Pastor Wysinger. He comes out of the church with two parishioners beside him. One, Jerry, I know from a large bear hunting group I've hunted with.

"Jerry, you know how this works, don't you?" I say as I hold up my Remington 870. He nods and grins broadly. I hand it to him and tell him no one is to come close to my van. He nods and checks the load as a true sportsman would.

I bear hug Reverend Wysinger before we head into his church. "Mark, you were right. Stragglers have been showin' up here since early this morning."

"Let's talk in private, Reverend," I say as we head into his office.

After closing the door to his office, the reverend opens up. "Mark, what you sent us from the Dollar General, that was God moving in you! How did you know? How did you know all these people would be coming through town?" he states questioningly.

"After our talk yesterday, I stopped at the Dollar General, I had the cash in hand and the clerk was willing to ring it up, so I figured to go for it, buy everything that could help these people. Probably a 'God Thing'." We both chuckle a bit, knowing that most people don't know that a "God Thing" happens to us all every day.

"Well, that was a heck of a 'God Thing' my friend!" the reverend responds.

"I guess you and Chief Wills have talked? He knows to send stragglers and other needy people here?"

"Yep. He was a little pissed at first, you buyin' up all that food for strangers, but then he figured out that movin' the stragglers along was best. But I'm a little worried about where they will end up."

"Same here, friend. We are sending these people down the road to who knows what? But can we offer them refuge here? What will that turn out to be? And I am sure that most of them still have no idea what has happened, and even if they do, they would still want to get home to their own families. At least try to."

"I keep thinking, God first, family second. But God first...treat others as you would have others treat you. That's a tough one. Some arrogant bastard already has demanded that we treat him as some noble figure. I basically told him to stand in line. But even with his boastfulness, I think we have to try and help him, help all of them."

"I feel your pain Brother Mark, I feel your pain. But most of these people, they want to move on, to get home. Let's help them to move on, like you said yesterday. Let's help to provide them with a means to move on. Your inspiration to do that is not against God's will. If they want to move on, let's help them to move on."

"You're right, Reverend. Let's help as we can. So we ought to see if some of these boys out there with the old trucks that still run, see if they can run some of these stragglers in towards Windber. I got no problem if the guys want to charge something to run them in, free rides lead to no good."

The reverend laughs, "No free rides! Mark! That's a good one, still got a sense of humor I see."

I laugh, too "Didn't mean it that way, but I guess you're right, or I'm right, no free rides!"

We both sit quietly reflecting on the joke that wasn't meant to be a joke, and how free rides have been such a bane on our society.

Bringing us back to the moment, I let the reverend know I need to head back into Johnstown to get my stepdaughter, her husband and their kids. I let him know that Becca knows my route and plans, not to worry about me. I also suggest that the community leaders need to meet within the next few days, the sooner the better, to figure out how we can make sure that our mountain community stays safe. He tells me he has no more information from our radio enthusiast. We talk a little more about the grave situation that the country faces. We agree that our best contribution will be to make sure that our small part of the country takes care of itself.

When we walk out to the church parking lot, we see even more people in line for the food and water, mainly stragglers, but a few local residents, too. There are also two more older farm trucks in the lot.

The reverend hollers over to the two boys with the farm trucks and starts talking with them about riding the stragglers into Windber. I hope that works out. But I need to get to the other side of Johnstown to get Britt, Kenny and the boys.

***

"Yo, Jerry," I holler. "You up for a little ride? Want to see how the city folk handled the grid being down?"

He is here to help the pastor, but with a nod from Reverend Wysinger, he agrees to go with me.

I holler over the small crowd that I am going to Roxbury, near the hospitals and I will take anyone going that way. A younger woman approaches and says that she wants to get her mom to the hospital, that her mom isn't doing well. We load them into the van. Two other couples ask for rides if it will take them closer to town.

We all head out of the church parking lot in my old van, past the stragglers and towards Johnstown, Jerry, riding shotgun, literally, with our passengers in the back. I ask Jerry if he is packing heat. He nods and pats his left side. I ask about spare clips, he indicates two. I'm liking Jerry, he is my kind of guy, concealed carry with spare clips.

I explain to Jerry my round-about, back country route to get to Johnstown. We both agree that avoiding the thousands of people at the Flight 93 Memorial is the best idea. So we skirt past Hooversville, and come in the back way to Davidsville. This puts us only a couple of miles from where my crew was working yesterday. It wasn't in my plans, but I have to go see if any of them are still there, if they left word as to where they were going. I explain to my passengers what's going on. They stare back blankly, still in shock. I make a left and a right, then a few hundreds yards later turn on the road where we are finishing up a large deck project.

I see my work van and Willis's truck. We pull up to the house, no signs of anyone home. I knock on the door and holler a few times. I look around back for a note, something. Willis, my lead carpenter has left a note scribbled on a piece of scrap wood. "Power out, nothing works. Waited for two hours, nothing works, van won't start, sent John home. We are both walking, call me. Willis." John, who is known as Herc, lives in Moxham. He is probably already home. Willis lives near Flight 93 Memorial, he will be walking into the crowds heading toward Johnstown. I have Jerry help me load some tools and supplies into the trailer from the jobsite that may be helpful later. I leave thousands of dollars in materials and dead equipment behind.

We head back the same way we came and end up coming in on the south end of Johnstown without significant incident. We do see a few trucks and older cars, some farm tractors and bicyclers. Many of the stalled cars have been pushed to the side of the road, some have people still with them, most have been left behind as their owners are now walking to their destinations. There are a lot of people walking. By the looks of them, the way they are dressed, most are Flight 93 stragglers, making their way to Johnstown.

Chapter 13 Hunting, November 2008

The shoosh, shoosh, shoosh of something walking through the fall leaves that lay heavy on the ground perks me up. My senses heighten once again. That is more than a squirrel scurrying from tree to tree. That is not a titmouse flitting about. That is a larger animal walking these woods.

I slowly turn towards the sound of the rustling leaves. I peer intently at the farthest sightlines I have; about two hundred yards to the fence line on the far side of the woods in front of me. I see movement! Three or more deer snooping along the fence line, just at the edge of my view. They are not moving fast, not being pushed. I bring my scoped 30.06 to bear on the area, adrenaline pumping. There are four or five deer. I move my scope from deer to deer. It is hard to keep track of which ones I have scoped and which ones may be a new deer as they mosey along, browsing. There is one stubborn deer trailing the rest that refuses to raise its head. 'That is the buck!' I think. But the deer refuses to raise his head as he skirts along the outer fringe of my safe shooting range. I jump my scope from deer to deer, looking for antlers: nothing. The group edges along, without revealing a target. I never got a good scope on all of them. The last one, he snuck by, staying low like a buck would. Well, I never had a good shot, never could identify him as a good target. I start to look elsewhere, maybe something walked up on my rear while I was watching the front! I settle back onto the stool in my tree stand and continue my vigilant watch.

Minutes later, the loud crack of a rifle shot echoes off the mountainsides. That was close! That was one of my brothers, or maybe Dad! My adrenaline spikes a bit again. My senses are at a peak as I strain my eyes to scan the woods in the direction that the shot came from; the same direction that the last group of deer headed towards. No second shot. That could be good, maybe the buck was taken on the first shot. Seconds pass and no second shot. Either a clean hit or clean miss. I wait in my tree stand, peering intently towards the area the shot came from, glancing around, trying to make sure that the buck, if missed, doesn't get past me.

Minutes pass. No sound or sight of any movement. I take one last minute to look all around for any sign of deer; no movement anywhere. Still keeping a wary eye out, I sling my rifle and make sure I have my knife, rope, water bottle, and spare rags in my game pouch. Whoever's shot was close, time to go see who it was and help out, especially if it was Dad. Can't have him hauling a dear a half-mile back to camp by himself.

I start heading up the slight rise to my Dad's deer stand, which is about a quarter mile away. I turn a slight bend in the path through the saplings that grow thick in this area. I see my dad bent over what is obviously a good buck.

"Got him, huh!" I holler out as I pick up my pace.

"Oh yeah, and he's a good one," my dad says as he looks towards me smiling. "Ten point, came trotting up the far fence line trailing four does. Stopped about a hundred yards from me and gave me the perfect shot, full broad side. He was sniffing for those does. Dropped him right here. He had to have come right past you. You didn't see him?"

Deer hunters love to talk about deer hunting; about the deer they saw, the deer they didn't see, the deer they shot, and the deer they didn't shoot. We can talk for fifteen minutes about all the deer we didn't see! So I tell Dad all about the deer I saw and the deer I didn't see, he tells me about all the deer he didn't see but the one he saw and shot! It's good camaraderie, the times you remember, the times you miss.

Meanwhile we get to gutting the deer. It is a good one, a ten point, twenty-four inch spread with a thick main beam and nine inch tines. The best deer Dad has ever shot. The best deer we have taken on the farm. "I knew this one was out here," Dad says. "I saw him at the feeder a few times last winter, a big eight point then. And he showed up on John's trail cams too. When I saw him come trotting in, Wow! He was dead set on following those does. He stopped not eighty yards from me, broadside. Look at that rack, Mark, look at those tines. We're going to get this one mounted. This is the one that goes over the fireplace."

"You gotta get that past Mom, ya know. She's pretty adamant about no dead animals on the wall."

"We'll get this buck mounted and stick it up there until we can take it to Canada. She may change her mind." Dad is referring to our family vacation place, which has lots of dead animals on the wall, mostly trophy fish.

***

The weekend had started with Thanksgiving dinner at Mom and Dad's. The kids and grandkids, those that are still in western PA, make the gathering about twenty strong. Lorrie, Becca, Jan and Eve take care of most of the cooking. My Mom wants to be a part of it all, but at eighty-two, she can't keep up with all that needs done, and is happy that her wisdom and traditions have been passed along. She supervises and smiles as the dinner is cooked and served. Before the large turkey is carved we all join hands and bow our heads as we say grace. Paul, the eldest, leads us, giving thanks to God for such a strong family, strong parents, and the blessings God has granted us all. He ends by saying the Lord's Prayer, and we all join in.

Large family gatherings at the Mays house usually include conversations ranging from the Pittsburgh Steelers, to church happenings and events, to what the grandkids are doing, to national and world politics. The conversation is bright and brisk. Some espouse rather verbally, some break the passion with quiet words of wisdom. Smaller side conversations grow. The happy bantering of a loving family celebrating a holiday is music to my mother's ears. She knows her mission here on earth has been completed.

I walk over to my mom, sitting in the large wing-backed chair, and sit beside her on the couch. Her eyes are glistening and her smile is joyful.

"You look very happy, Mom, almost glowing."

"I am very happy, Mark. My children know the Lord, and I will see them all in heaven. I cannot be happier!" She smiles and looks at me. "And you, Mark, you were a lost soul, so much talent that God blessed you with. But you figured it out. It took you twenty years, twenty years of praying for you. And look at you now, you are just beginning to grow. God has a plan for you, Mark. Follow his plan."

"I know, Mom. I know now you prayed for me, just as I pray daily for my kids and grandkids. I'm sorry I put you and Dad through such torment. But I guess that was the path I needed to follow. I know better now. My selfish days are over. My heart is with the Lord, and I am glad you know that." Mom and I reminisce a bit, glossing over the stupid things, of which there are many, and dwelling on the good things.

As the gathering is breaking up, I pull John aside. "You're staying overnight, aren't you?"

"Yeah. Dad wants us to check all the deerstands and walking trails. I want to take a few shots with my rifle and Jan and I are going to do some pistol practice."

"Okay, cool, Becca and I will be out before noon. We picked up a few cool new weapons, I want you and Jan to see them. Trust me, you are going to want to put some rounds down range!" John looks at me a little quizzically, but is quickly caught up in another conversation about the recent presidential election.

***

Becca and I show up the next morning just in time for the last round of blueberry pancakes and sausage. Dad wants to make sure that all the treestand repairs are done before we sight in our guns. The three men head out and take care of Dad's must do fixes. John inquires about why shooting will be so fun today. I just smile and keep silent, letting the suspense build.

John is the marksman of the family. He has the best target group every time we shoot. He brings a group from his church out to the farm every summer, ages eight to eighty-eight, to train them in handgun firing and safety. He is not just an NRA member, he is active in teaching responsible gun ownership. He is a gun enthusiast, despite Jan's pacifist nature.

We have a great range area set up, shooting into the embankment of the large pond. We have a pistol range that allows us to shoot from up to fifty feet away. There are five lanes set up that we can pin a basic target to. There is a long table sixty feet back from the targets for reloading and cleaning. We keep the area mowed between the bench and the targets so it is easy to walk from the firing area to the targets. We also have a one-hundred yard range for our deer rifles with two firing lanes and a smaller bench. Because of the lay of the land, with the slight rise toward the pond embankment, we could sight in from five hundred yards if we wanted to.

At the pistol range, we have Jan and Becca fire a couple clips at the targets, tin cans from twenty feet. They reluctantly fire the weapons, showing they know how, but complaining that they have to do this every year. John and I burn thru a few more clips, just to stay rehearsed with each handgun

We drive out to the hundred yard range and set up to fire our deer rifles, both Remington 30.06's. John shoots first and puts all three shots within two inches of the "10" mark. Good by him, good by me. I shoot three rounds. Basically good, but a little high. I make a few slight scope adjustments and fire three more times. Two shots close to the "10" ring, one four inches off center. I know my shooting, I am not a sniper, I shoot okay, so this grouping works for me.

"So, what's all the secrecy, Mark? You said you had something new to shoot, something cool. You got two new hard cases there, what's inside 'em?"

I pull both cases out of the back of Dad's old farm truck and begin to open them up. "John, you and I have been talking for years about getting a few good self defense guns, but the time was never right, the price was never right. With this past presidential election and the economic downturn that is starting, this banking meltdown, I felt the time was right. I think our new president is an honest man. And when he says he's worried about those that cling to their Bibles and their guns, I believe him!"

I have both cases laying side by side on the tailgate of the truck, latches released but still unopened. I dramatically flip both cases open at the same time revealing two identical Colt AR15 M4-style semi-automatic rifles. I had cleaned and oiled both, so they look almost brand new.

"No," says John. "Sweet!" He actually gets a little flushed in the face. I nod towards the weapons as I pull out the one nearest me. He gently picks up the other one.

Jan and Becca are silent as we check over the weapons. An AR15 is similar in action to the M16A1 I was trained on except it will only shoot semiautomatic, one shot every time you pull the trigger; no fully automatic mode. I show John the mechanics of the weapon, also having Jan and Becca go through all the drills of safety, firing, jams and reloading.

I was able to pick up both weapons, ten extra clips and a little under two thousand rounds of ammunition for a very good price. One of the guys who works for me, he got the lead that a guy was in trouble paying his mortgage, so I got both weapons and rounds at a fire sale price. I felt a bit conflicted after I bought the guns at such a bargain, but I am a free market capitalist; I paid him what he asked, after a bit of dickering. Hopefully he was able to right his own financial ship.

We all move up to the fifty-yard stake on the target lanes and John and I begin the systematic procedure of sighting in the guns. We find the standard iron sights are true. Quickly, we move on to setting up cans to see how fast we can knock them down. We bring both girls in on the fun, and after they get the hang of it, they find knocking down cans in quick succession to be more exhilarating than they thought. We back up to the hundred yard mark and do it all over again. John can consistently hit the target, the girls and I can too, sometimes!

After more than two hours since we left the house, we return; all of us smiling and talking about the good time we just spent together, learning each others strengths and weaknesses, overcoming misplaced phobias, growing as brothers and sisters, even as adults.

Chapter 14 Moxham Burning, September 12, 2018

As Jerry and I approach the little town known as Ben's Creek, I can see that a checkpoint has been set up. We pull off to the side of the road, a couple of hundred yards short of the roadblock.

"I don't want to roll up on that checkpoint without seeing what's going on," I state. "Jerry, step out and look around. See if you can get a feel for what's going on up there. I'm going to scope them out a bit." I pull out my Pentax 8 x 40 binoculars that my wife gave me many years ago and start to study the checkpoint and the surrounding terrain.

The roadblock looks pretty harmless, even helpful. It's set up in front of a large Catholic church. They seem to have an aid and supply station set up similar to what we did in Central City. There looks to be a food line set up and some people handing out water and providing directions and information. I don't see anyone being detained or harassed.

"Looks like St Francis' has set up an aid station." I say to Jerry.

"Looks pretty kosher to me, too," Jerry responds. "But look at those smoke plumes."

Taking down the binocs, I look at where Jerry is pointing. There are at least three large fires burning and several small fires. One of the large smoke plumes could be coming from where Janie saw the fuel truck catch the hillside on fire. I can't tell where the others may be coming from, but there are several obviously big fires burning. This is not good. Many homes in Johnstown were built well over a hundred years ago. There are many abandoned and blighted homes. A large fire could raze entire blocks, even entire neighborhoods, without an active fire department. And I doubt very much that the firetrucks were hardened against an EMP.

Again, I say a silent prayer. Again, I ask God why. But it is obvious why. Like the Israelites who turned away from God time and time again, we have turned away from God. Freedom of religion has been turned into freedom from religion. Our country's founding, based on Old Testament scriptures, has been debased and ridiculed. Faith has been ridiculed as extreme, while immorality, entitlement and greed have been praised.

"Our God is a loving God," I say out loud, "Until you turn your back on him, piss him off." I think of 'Pissed Christ' and shake my head.

"Okay, everyone." I say loud enough for our passengers to hear, "We are going to roll up to this roadblock. Some of you may want out there. It looks like an aid and supply effort. I'm going about a mile further into town, which will be closer to the hospital. But as you can see, a lot of smoke is coming up from town. There are at least two or three big fires. You all can decide what to do when we get up to the church's aid station."

Jerry loads back in and we head down to the checkpoint. A couple of locals stop us, both armed with long guns.

"Hey, friend," I state as a middle-aged man steps up to my window. "I need to get to Roxbury, to get my daughter and grandkids. We also got a few people here who would like to get to the hospital or through town to the airport. What's it look like up that way?"

He looks us over, a bit grimly but with no ill will. "It's clear up to the hospital. But more people are being taken out of there than are going in. All the systems are shut down and they can't do much more than emergency procedures, like stitches and burns. Gettin' through the city would be a pipe dream. Big fire in Moxham, nothing going to stop it, unless it rains. People are fleeing across the river and up the hill. I wouldn't advise going that way, liable to lose your vehicle in the panic. We got some of their residents here now, and they say it's pretty bad, everyone for themselves."

"We just came in from Central City, took the back roads. You got several thousand people heading this way from the Flight 93 Memorial, but most of them should end up in Richland. God bless you all for setting up this aid station. Is it okay for us to pull over up ahead, so my passengers can decide what to do?" He nods and we pull off up the road a bit.

The woman with the ailing mother wants to get her to the hospital, so she will ride on with us. One of the couples is from New Jersey and they want to try and get home, despite the odds against that. They have children there and are petrified at this point. They are still clinging to the hope that they can fly home or get a bus. We let them off here at the church, as there is some aid and they can get a game plan together.

The last couple are in their fifties and childless. Their home is in upstate New York, and they came to the Flight 93 Memorial as a bucket list thing. They now realize how hopeless it is to get home. He is a mechanical engineer and she is a retired schoolteacher. They ask about returning to Central City with us. They let us know they are willing to help in anyway they can. These two are intelligent people, they have not been demanding, more hopeful than anything. I make a gut decision and agree to help them out.

***

We proceed into town, to my stepdaughter's house, dropping off the daughter and mom about a quarter mile from the hospital. From Britt's house, high on the hill, we are overlooking Moxham. A large fire is burning. It has consumed about four blocks and is spreading. We see people moving across the bridges, heading away from the danger. We see people gathering at the high school stadium. It is chaos in slow motion. We can hear the occasional gunshot and boom as something blows up. Looking through the binocs, I see an older car get stopped by three people with guns. I see three people in the car get shot and pulled from the car. I see the three thugs jump in the car and head off--anarchy.

Moxham is a beautiful old neighborhood of Johnstown. It is named after the founder of Moxham Steel, which later became part of Bethlehem Steel that helped build America. The history is rich and the homes are diverse and beautiful. There are the mansions built by the Moxham family high on the bluff. There are beautiful homes on almost every corner with the original detailed woodwork and gingerbread porches. These would have been the homes of the foremen, engineers and accountants. Mixed in are the row homes of the workers. Some singles homes, some double homes. If these homes weren't in a blighted neighborhood in Johnstown, they would sell for hundreds of thousands of dollars, maybe even be put on the list of historical homes.

But the steel industry collapsed, and the jobs left, and these beautiful homes fell into disrepair. Yesterday these three-story, four-bedroom houses with exquisite woodwork could be bought for a song. Today they are worth nothing and burning to the ground.

This entire neighborhood was built over one hundred years ago, from the vast Pennsylvania forests. The row homes are only five to ten feet apart so the fire quickly jumps from home to home with nothing to stop it. There are also trees over one hundred years old that line the streets. Trees so large they form a canopy over the streets which also forms a bridge for the fire to jump the street when the trees are consumed by the intense heat.

It is surreal. From high on the bluff, I am watching this inferno, violence and chaos. The strong sunlight from the east, mixed with the heavy plumes of smoke from the fires, combine to make an eerie and oppressive sight.

As I scan the area, I see something odd. It seems to have been a tree falling down. Through the binocs I search the area more thoroughly. I can see several trees have been cut down, and limbed, and the limbs are being hauled away. There are work crews! Firemen, neighbors, friends, whoever, are working together to cut a fire block! That could work; I pray that it works. I think that Herc, my steady worker, is leading one of those work crews, helping to save his neighborhood, helping to save his home and family.

Despite the fact that there are no firetrucks, I can see that the firemen have hauled their hoses from the Hornerstown firehouse and are spraying down what they can. Johnstown's water system is fed by the Quemahoning Dam, which is high in the mountains. The steel mills used over ten million gallons a day when they were operating. The water pressure and supply will be strong, despite the power outage; electricity doesn't affect gravity. Despite the violence and chaos around them, a group of people have banded together to stop the destruction of the fire. Praise God! The entire scene is unnerving. One of my best workers lives down there. His family lives down there. It is too much to comprehend.

I refocus on the mission at hand when Britt, Kenny and their kids come running out of their home and embrace us. Britt is in tears. "Oh my God, you have to get us out of here!" she exclaims. "Look, freaking Moxham is on fire!" she says, pointing over the hill, "It's been a freakin' war down there all night! Let's get this old heap loaded up and get out of here. Come on boys, load up the trailer and van. Now! Now! Now!"

Linc, the engineer, and his wife, Kim, the school teacher, stand mesmerized by what they are seeing. A small town in the middle of America is burning to the ground and violence is taking place before their eyes. What would Rochester be like now, they wonder. What about Philadelphia and New York? They realize even more that going home right now is not an option. I get them started on helping to load the trailer and van as bins and luggage are brought out by the kids.

"Britt," I say to my stepdaughter, as she comes out with another bin of clothes, "You all may never get back here again. Make sure you grab stuff that you will really miss. We have food and all that. Make sure you grab pictures and the like."

"You old freak! That's already been loaded. Get with the program, old man! Step it up! I don't want to be around here when the crazy shit happening down there gets up here!"

That's my wife's daughter, semi-hysterical, but totally in control. I help with the loading and strapping down while a few neighbors look on. Kenny talks with the neighbors to let them know he and the family are bugging out to Central City. At my suggestion he lets them know to use anything in the house that might help them get through this chaos, but to also keep an eye on the house, keep strangers away.

As Britt and the boys are doing a final check of the house and what's been loaded, the newly formed foursome of men walk back over and look down on the Moxham section of the city. A clear firebreak can be seen forming up Ohio Street where the trees are being cut down. It looks as if another firebreak is being cut to save the homes higher on the bluff. We can see people streaming away from the fire ravaged area. It is chaos, but a more controlled chaos than I expected.

Chapter 15   Returning Home, September 12, 2018

As we head back out of town, we are a little more loaded down than I expected to be. We have eight people. Me driving, Jerry riding shotgun, Linc and Kim, our rescued stragglers, and Britt, Kenny, Larson and Grace, as well as a fully loaded trailer, and travel bags strapped to the roof.

We pull up to the checkpoint at Bens Creek on Route 403. The men there remember us from a few hours earlier. I request to pull aside again, so I can talk with them a bit about what's going on in town. They agree to that, eager for reliable information. I suggest they bring over the pastor or whoever is in charge.

I let Jerry know he is in charge and not to let anyone near the van. Kenny, Britt and Linc step out also, and though unarmed, take up guard positions. I grab an AR 15 out of the back and hand it to Kenny. A little shocked, he checks the load and safety, then stands ready. I smile grimly, he smiles back. He's a city boy, but he is a Boy Scout, literally.

I walk over to where one of the checkpoint guards stands with another middle-aged man. He is nicely dressed, but his clothes are dirty and disheveled. It's been a long day for this man.

"I'll try to be brief, friend. I can see you have your hands full, but good information will be key, since we have no phones or radios. I thought you might want to hear what I saw, no rumors, no bullshit." He nods for me to go on. "It was clear from here to the park, but a lot of people are walking and riding bikes, a couple of old cars and trucks were on the road too. I picked my kids up on the bluff overlooking Moxham. It's bad down there. I saw some people get shot and car jacked. Several blocks are on fire, and the fire is jumping the streets over the tree canopy. There are several work crews cutting down trees on Ohio Street to make a fire break. They also seemed to be working across Highland or Cypress to stop the fire from moving up the bluff. Many people are crossing the bridges to Ferndale and Hornerstown. They are probably showing up here already. More seem to be heading to Hornerstown and Kernville. It looks like an aid station has been set up at Trojan Stadium, a lot people are congregating there."

"Any sign of the police or fire department?" he asks.

"Yeah, it looked like the fire department walked in from the Hornerstown Station with hoses and are trying to slow the fire down. No sign of police anywhere, not to say they weren't there, just no cars with lights.

"The woods above Moxham are on fire, too. That's heading up towards Belmont, it's a big fire. There was also a fire in Kernville or downtown, I couldn't tell which. I hope it's lower Kernville, less buildings to burn as most have already been torn down. It will burn out quickly.

"They were also flying people out of Murtha Airport yesterday, but that has stopped as far as I know."

The well dressed, but worn down, man sizes me up. He looks me in the eye. "You know more than most. You are working on what you know, not rumor and bullshit. I can see that. Tell me what you know, what the hell is going on here," he asks forlornly, almost pleadingly.

"Armageddon, and there was no Rapture, my brother." I state. "God has showed his displeasure with us. America has been attacked. Nuclear I am sure. High altitude electro-magnetic-pulse device, EMP, knocked out everything electrical or electronic. I have heard that there were ground level nukes too. We are in world war three. I am sure we retaliated, so nothing works anywhere. Don't expect FEMA or the Armed Services or any national government agency to be riding in to help out. They're shut down too. That's more my opinion thn fact, but it's the best answer I can give you."

The man looks at me, then looks down and shakes his head. "I have to go," he says, "I have to go." He slowly turns and walks away. Several people come up to him, asking questions, tugging at him for attention. He keeps plodding aimlessly across the parking lot, ignoring their pleas for help, for guidance. He can only get guidance from above at this point. He is not the first one to be overwhelmed by what has happened, and he certainly won't be the last.

I turn to the checkpoint guard. "Pray with him, comfort him if you can. Remember what I just told you and tell the people who need to know. Things may be bad now, but they are going to get worse. Even good people will start to get violent when they start to get hungry. And with the grid being down, that's going to happen very soon."

He looks at me with determination in his eyes, but also a look of bewilderment. He looks lost, seeing a parishioner that he looked up to so defeated. I hug him compassionately and whisper to him that God will be with him. These are words that have come to me easily over my many years of faith and trials, and I still believe them now. I think briefly of our brethren Christians in the Middle East and the persecution they faced against the Taliban and ISIS, and how I used to pray for faith such as theirs. That test is coming now. I again pray that I have faith that strong.

I head back towards our van. Britt, Kenny, Linc and Jerry still stand guard, determined looking, but not threatening. Twenty-four hours in and they get the gravity of the situation. They have seen a neighborhood on fire and seen or heard the gunfire. They know this is serious and to keep alert.

"Time to go guys. Kenny, keep that AR handy." We load up and head back towards the farmstead. Just like the day before, we see some older trucks, cars and motorcycles; for the most part they are as loaded down as we are. But a few seem to be out joy riding, partying it up. Firearms are visible everywhere. Riding shotgun is no longer just a phrase from the past. In the hills of western Pennsylvania, where 'we cling to our guns and our Bibles,' I worry some don't have the Bible with them anymore.

***

State Route 403 winds along the valley of the Stoney Creek River for about ten miles between Hollsopple and Hooversville, crossing the river a few times. It is a good road, but seldom traveled, except by locals. A few of the Flight 93 stragglers have figured out that it's a shorter walking route with less hills than taking Route 30 to 219. They must have been the few with a real map, because GPS is no longer working. We pass several groups heading the opposite way, towards Johnstown. They look tired and desperate. Some try to flag us down, but I can't help them.

I get an idea. I pull off the road along an open stretch and go to the back of the van. There are still a few cases of water there from the day before. I set one out on the side of the road and jump back in. It's not much, but I hope it helps out someone.

As I get back in the van, an older truck barrels down the road from the opposite direction. The driver veers into my lane and lays on the horn, nearly hitting my door as I jump back in the van. I see the driver clearly laughing as he passes. Four guys in the back are hooting and hollering. One takes some pots shots at us with a semi- automatic rifle. I hear a couple of thunks and Grace screams out in pain.

"Son of a bitch!" I yell. "Britt, Grace's been hit, check on him. Jerry, there's a first aid kit under your seat. We got to get going before those hyped-up bastards come back."

"Sonna bitch! Assholes shot my son! Sonna bitchin' assholes! Kenny, you better know how to use that gun you got there!" Britt is in full mother hen mode, already turned in the seat and checking out her younger son.

"It's my arm, Mom, it's my arm," Grace grits. "My left arm, oh that friggin' hurts."

I keep looking in my rearview mirror to see if these hyped-up bastards are coming back. As I do we cross the first bridge across the Stoneycreek River. Before I can even think to slow down we pass four people on the side of the road, shot dead from the looks of it, blood still spreading on the road. Not good, those hyped-up evil bastards have already got the taste of blood, anarchy, no retaliation for their evil deeds. Not good.

As we come off the turn from the bridge, I hit the gas. Eight people, a trailer and a loaded van, we slowly gain speed. It's four miles to the next town where the thought of all the people around may cause these country junkies to hold off.

***

I say country junkies, because drugs is by no means only an inner-city problem. And I'm not talking about some weed here. Meth has been a serious problem for decades, but what has finally come to light is that heroin addiction in small town America is rampant. Hopelessness has led to despair, which has led to drugs.

Our federal government has set in place regulations and tax policies that have killed manufacturing and small businesses in our country. So when kids graduate from high school, or even college, they have no future. They can't get a job in the factory or the mill or the mine, because there aren't any more factories, mills or mines. So with no future, too many young men and women turn to government dependence and drugs, inner-city Baltimore or rural Pennsylvania, it's the same story.

These boys that shot at us are meth heads. Heroin addicts generally want to be left alone. They don't cause trouble until they need more money for their next hit. That's when they'll kill their own mom for twenty bucks. Unfortunately, we have seen that happen right in our back yard.

***

Still watching to our rear, I see a truck scream off the bridge and head up behind us.

"Kenny, Jerry, here they come. Everyone get down! Now!" Last second thinking has me pull over to the left lane, that forces them to pull back to the right lane and pass us unexpectedly on the right. No shots are fired as I see bodies and guns jostling in the back of the truck from the unexpected maneuver.

There is a sharp turn and bridge about two miles ahead, to cross the river again, about a mile before Hooversville, and maybe safety. We saw the last group of shot-up people on a bridge. I pull over. Time to think this out.

"Britt, you got Grace bandaged up?"

"As best I can for now, those friggin' assholes shot him in the arm! I got the bleeding stopped but he needs stitches."

"Okay, guys, we have to cross another bridge about two miles up the road. These meth heads are going to be sitting there. My guess is, they shot up those folks we saw at the last bridge. They already got a sense of anarchy, the smell of blood. Going around will send us smack into the Flight 93 crowd and we will not get through that without losing the van and everything we carry. That's not an option. We got to showdown with these meth heads."

"Mark! They already shot Grace, and they killed those people we passed!" Britt says vehemently. "We can't go through them, find another way!"

"That's not an option, Britt, we have to take these crazy bastards out. We have to set up a plan to cross that bridge."

"We can do this, Mark," comes a voice from the back. "I saw you got your Remington 700 with a 3 x 12 scope in the back. If they are standing open on that bridge, I can shoot them," Kenny calmly states from the back seat. "I know the bridge you're talking about. Get me within two hundred yards and I can shoot them. It's a clear path, I know, because of the drop off to the river."

I turn around and look at Kenny, always nice and kind "Kenny". He looks at me, his face gets hard, his lips turn grim, his eyes narrow. "They shot my son." I have never heard words spoken with such determination and dark passion. "I've shot competition, I can shoot them."

His eyes are so hard, there is no way I can say no. We make a plan. Ken will be on the roof of the van, nestled in the luggage. We will pull to within two hundred yards. I will get out and offer them peace, but let them know they have drawn blood and we mean business. Jerry will have the shotgun and Britt will have the AR in the back seat. She has shot it before and we give her a quick refresher course. If we have to run the bridge, we will. We figure they can only block the middle. We will run it on the left and deal with any injuries and damage to the van later.

We pull up another mile and the bridge comes in sight. I pull up to about two hundred yards short of the bridge. The truck is sitting there, pulled across the bridge, mainly across the right hand lane. I step out of the van, staying behind the door for at least some minimal protection. Without looking up, I ask Kenny if he has a clear view.

"Got 'em," he states tersely.

"Yo to the bridge!" I holler. "We need to get to Central City, we need to cross this bridge."

"You have to pay a toll to cross the bridge." A large man bellows back. We hear some distant snickering and laughing.

"What's the toll?" I holler.

"I have them scoped," Kenny says from atop the van "I can hit four of them from here."

"Your women, to start!" responds the large man.

"You already took some of my grandson's blood. I ain't takin' too kindly to anymore negotiatin'. Move your vehicle now and all is forgiven."

I hear a gunshot and a tink as it ricochets off the pavement, five feet to my left.

"Son-of-a-bitch!" I exclaim as I hear the 30-06 boom from the top of the van. The shooter drops to the road. Before I can say anything else, the 30-06 booms three more times. The talker, and the two in the back of the truck drop, too. The one that was still standing in the road, and the driver that was still in the truck, are already running. The loud report rings one more time, and the one who was driving drops to the ground also.

Ken climbs down from the top of the van, grimness expressed across his face. He deliberately reloads the rifle as he gets in the van. Britt looks at him, half horrified, half with

122

respect and adoration. I am sure the adoration is going to overtake the horrified part. A man did what he had to do to protect his family. That is to be admired. They drew first blood, and tried to draw second blood even when we offered peace. I have a clear conscience. I hope Ken does, too.

I glance at Ken as I get in. There is a steely distant stare in his eyes. Not sinister, but harsh, angry. He doesn't look at anyone, not me, not his kids, not even his wife. He just stares blankly ahead.

I put the van in gear and slowly head towards the bridge. The tension in the van is stifling. I begin reciting out loud, from memory "The Lord is my Shepherd, I shall not want. He makes melie down in green pastures, He leads me beside still waters." Others in the van join in as best they can. "He restores my soul, and leads me in the paths of righteousness. Yea, though I walk through the valley of the shadow of death, I will fear no evil, for thou art with me, thy rod and thy staff comfort me. Thou prepare a table before me in the presence of my enemies. Thou anoint my head with oil, my cup runneth over. Surely goodness and mercy shall follow me all of my days, and I will dwell in the house of the Lord forever." We finish the 23rd Psalm together, a bit disjointedly. I don't know where that came from. I have not recited the whole psalm in over 40 years. We all know parts of it. Many recite it in Sunday school as kids. But, the Lord moves us when needed. I glance in the mirror. Ken is sobbing, everyone is crying. Tears are rolling down my cheeks, too.

As we cross the bridge, I make a few swerves around the bodies, two are still alive. Some in the van are staring at the men on the ground, some are deliberately staring straight out the front window. I can see that Jerry is scanning for threats. I start to think he is a veteran, maybe the Persian Gulf in 1992.

"Stop!" Ken commands as we finish crossing the bridge, passing the truck and the men he just shot. "We have to help them. At least two are still alive. We can't just leave them here."

"Ken, we can't!" I say. "These guys are killers! We can let someone in Hooversville know and they can come clean this up, if they want to."

"No, Mark, we'll clean it up. I'll clean it up. Stop now." And I stop.

"Slow up there, Ken," says Jerry. "One of them ran off and we don't know if these guys are still armed. Let's move real slow, and be ready if one of them pulls a handgun. I'll stand watch. Mark, you and Ken go see what you can do. Check the driver for keys to the truck, we'll use that to carry them."

"I'm going with you," says Linc. A quick look at his determined face lets me know not to argue. I hand him my 9mm as I grab my AR15. Ken looks at me and grabs the other AR15. His eyes have dried, and I can see he is already thinking more clearly, but he is probably still in shock from what he just did.

***

I check the pulse on the first one we come to. I have never looked at a dead body. He is lying on his back, shot in the chest, center mass. He is lying in a pool of blood. I turn away quickly after stepping in his sticky blood and feeling his already cold neck. I dry heave for several seconds, but my stomach is empty. My eyes water to the point that I can't see. I hear someone else retching, too. As I clear my eyes I see that it is Linc. Ken comes over and gives me a hand up from my knees. His face is ashen and he has tears in his eyes again, but also a grim look of determination.

Regaining my composure, I look at him and say, "Thanks, sorry 'bout that. Let's get on with this." Jerry has walked over to us, while still keeping an eye out, and hands us each a bottle of water. I gladly slug down half a bottle, trying to rid myself of the taste of bile in my mouth. Jerry returns to the van and stands guard as we continue on.

We don't stop to check the pulse of the second body, no need to. He was the first one shot, through the head, lying in a pool of blood. The next one is breathing, lying on his back, clutching his upper abdomen, dark blood oozing through his fingers. I get queasy again but manage to keep from heaving. He's trying to say something but he can't, no words come from his barely moving lips. We keep moving on, almost trance-like. How can we help the man? What can we do? We all seem to know without saying anything that he is already dead, bleeding out on the road, shot through the liver.

The fourth man is dead too, another center mass chest shot. We pass him by. We are coming up to the driver, who ran. He is trying to pull himself along, trying to get off to the side of the road. He is gut shot. He looks at us with terror in his eyes.

"I'm sorry man! I didn't mean no harm. I was just out ridin' with the boys, and with all the craziness going on… I'm sorry, it just got out of control. Help me! Please! Help me."

"We're going to help you," says Ken. "We'll take you to Hooversville. Hopefully there's a doctor there who can help you. We need the keys to your truck so we can take you there."

"No! Not Hooversville!" the young man exclaims. "Take me to Johnstown, they won't like me in Hooversville. I don't think they'll help me. You gotta take me to Johnstown. Or Windber! You can take me to Windber, please! But not Hooversville! They won't help me there."

"I got the keys, they're in the truck," hollers Link. "I'll back it over there."

Moments later I lower the tailgate and my eyes open a bit wide. Ken looks in too. "Whoa! These boys were ready for world war three!" He exclaims.

"Linc, the bed is full of guns and ammo. Back this thing up to the van so we can get it unloaded." I holler. We quickly load up ammo cans and weapons, some liquor and a couple cases of beer, too. I don't even try to figure out what all is there. I want to get moving before more people come along.

We load the four dead bodies in first, then the driver, who is still alive. Jerry hollers that a group of stragglers are coming down the road and we should get moving. We have Linc drive the pickup with Ken as shotgun. Jerry and I load back into the van. I leave what's left of our last case of water in the middle of the road for the stragglers heading this way. What are they going to think? I wonder. They had to have heard the shooting, saw us load these bodies into the truck, and now they'll find a case of water amidst this grisly scene of still fresh pools of blood.

***

The ladies and kids start asking questions as we get started down the road. We try to answer them as best as possible. The group of stragglers tries to string across the road to stop us. I lay on the horn and step on the gas. They move. We left them water. There is not much more I can do. That commotion quiets everyone down. We climb a large hill just before we get to Hooversville, and as we crest the hill, we see another roadblock. This is not a checkpoint like the one next to the church in Bens Creek. This is four vehicles across the road with armed men, tense and angry by the looks of it. We pull over a hundred yards short of the roadblock.

"Yo to the roadblock, we mean no harm and wish to travel to Central City." I holler.

"That's the truck!" I hear someone yell. Whoa, not good.

"Hey, you drugged out killin' bastards" someone else yells and I see firearms being raised.

Lord, be with me! I step from behind the door and wave my hands above my head, a universal distress signal. I wish I had a white towel, but no time for that now.

"Stop! Stop! Stop! Peace! Peace! Peace!" I yell as loud as I can. "That ain't us! Stop! Stop! Stop! Peace! Peace! Peace!"

I see weapons lowered a bit at my frantic yelling and waving. 'Thank you, Lord!' I don't think they expected to see a short-haired, gray bearded man yelling Peace!

"I know what you mean about that truck behind me!" I yell. "They attacked us, too." No wonder the guy didn't want to go to Hooversville. "We dealt with them, let me approach, I am unarmed." I see a few of them talking amongst themselves, some of it agitated, animated, some of it calm. A man about my age steps forward, and lets me know to come forward.

I walk on up and we meet about twenty-five yards from their roadblock. I extend my hand and say, "Mark Mays, from Central City."

"Chris Speigle, Fire Chief," he responds, shaking my hand firmly. "That truck back there, it's been shootin' up the town. They robbed the bank, the pharmacy and two bars. At least eight people been killed by them. What do you mean you dealt with 'em? You almost got shot, but for your crazy antics!"

"They tried shootin' us up too, then they set an ambush for us." I say. "But we dealt back better than they could give out." I look to the sky and say sincerely, "Thank you, Lord." Looking back at Chris I say. "Four of them are dead in the back of the truck, one was still alive, but he is gut shot. Pleaded with me not to take him here, now I know why.

"I got my family with me that I picked up in Johnstown this morning and we're trying to get back to my farm in Central City. Johnstown is a mess, shootin's and several big fires. Came this way to avoid the crowds stuck at the Flight 93 Memorial. Walk back with me and you can check us over."

He sizes me up, wisely. He turns back to the men at the roadblock, "This man here says they dealt with the Wagerlys, that they're dead in the truck. I'm going out to check things over. You all stay calm, but keep alert. And don't let none of them stragglers through 'til we get this cleared up. If them Wagerlys are still out there, them stragglers will get kilt, sure as daylight."

We walk together out to our little caravan. I tell him about the drive-by shooting, the dead stragglers and our final run-in on the last bridge. When we get to the truck, he looks in the bed. The driver is still alive. He looks at Chris, "No! No! Chris! I didn't know that was Jennifer! I'm so sorry! I told you not to take me to Hoovers…" BANG! He didn't get out the last word as Chris has shot him in the head with his 357 S&W revolver.

I jump back, Jerry jumps out with his AR15, and Ken jumps out, too.

"Calm down, everyone!" Chris bellows with authority, as he sees armed men emerge from the van and truck. "Jennifer was my daughter," he says softly. We lower our weapons. He turns, and starts walking back.

I can hear him sobbing softly, as he slowly makes his way down the road. I quickly catch up to him and put my arm around him. He turns to me slowly, tears rolling down his cheeks. I embrace him and he lets his weight fall on me, both physically and spiritually. He has lost a daughter, and now he feels as if he has lost his soul. I whisper to him that God is a graceful God, That God loves him even now. "I don't know if there is a God, Mark. I don't know if there is a God." He steps back and as he turns to head back down the road he says, "Bring your people up. You're okay."

I walk back to where Ken is standing, the steely distant stare is back. "You tried to do good, son, you tried to do good. Let it go. Your son was shot and survived. His daughter was killed by that man, many people were killed by those men. Let it go, Ken. You did the right thing, a hard thing, but the right thing." He nods, his face unchanged, and turns to get in the truck. I load up and we pull up to the roadblock.

***

At the roadblock, I tell everyone to stay in the van except Jerry, who steps out with his shotgun held low but ready. Ken and Linc stay in the truck, Ken is still steely eyed.

"That's dem damn Wagerlys! Hot damn, man! Holy shit, you killed five of 'em!" exclaims a younger man as he looks in the bed of the truck. As he continues looking at the death and gore, his face turns ashen and he runs to the side of the road, heaving up his lunch, clutching his stomach.

An older man steps up to me, "So, Chris says you kilt five of them but one ran off into the woods. They robbed my bar, kilt my son and a good worker of mine." He turns and spits. "Those hyped-up boys were runnin' crazy. They used to drink at my place sometimes, but last night and this morning, they just started runnin' crazy." He shakes his head and spits again. "I never thought them boys was that bad, but they sure turned bad. Guess they figured wasn't no law to stop 'em. I gotta thank you, sir. They kilt my son. The power goes out and people turn bad, ain't right." He looks down and shakes his head. "We set up here and at the other end of town and up on Hill Road too. Needed to do something to stop 'em."

Chris, the fire chief, walks over with a few other men as the bar owner is talking. When the man finishes, I turn to Chris. "What do I do with these bodies? Can you and your men help us bury them?"

"We been talking bout that. They aint gettin' buried, not here, but we'll take 'em off the truck fer ya. We was wonderin' what ya found in the truck?" Chris asks.

I was kind of expecting this question, the truth is always the best answer. "We found several weapons, five or six rifles and shot guns and a few hand guns. There was also a lot of ammo and some liquor and beer. We loaded it into the van and trailer. I'll show ya, follow me."

"No need, friend," Chris responds. "We're not worried about the guns and ammo in your hands. We talked about it, and a well-armed friend is a good friend. How 'bout drugs? Did you find any drugs, pills, meth, heroin? We're more worried about that stuff."

"We didn't search for that kind of stuff. It could be under the seat, anywhere. Let's check it over while your men get the bodies off the truck. You seem to be playing the long game, letting us keeping the guns, Chris, you know what happened don't you?"

"EMP, nuclear attacks in DC and New York, Other EMPs across the world. Shit has hit the fan, Mark, but you know that already, too." He states matter of factly.

I nod. "You got someone with a working ham radio." A statement not a question. He nods. "We got a guy too, heard similar stuff. So why are we still here? Where is God? I understand your questions better now. I don't know the answers. But we are still here and God has a plan for us. We didn't meet by chance, Chris. This is part of His plan. And I'm happy to be your well-armed friend down the road."

I wave Jerry over and indicate to Ken for him to join us. Chris has his men bring over a front end loader and they start unloading the bodies. Ken helps them search the truck for any drugs we may have missed. The bar owner asks about any more liquor and we determine they must have dropped that at their camp. They had cleaned his place out of booze and as much beer as they could load. We also determine that there must be several more meth heads in their group. Chris says they'll make plans to pay their camp a visit. Jerry offers them some simple but prudent advice about their roadblocks. We get one of Chris's EMTs to tend to Grace's arm. Fortunately he has some antibiotics for him, too.

The search of the truck comes up with some small amounts of meth, a couple of packets of heroin, and a few used needles, but no large stashes of prescription grade pills, or opiatess. This means that there must be a significant stash of drugs at their compound. The pharmacist, and her technician, were both killed, so no one knows how much the Wagerlys got away with. I want to ask about meds that I know Becca and James will need, but I hold my tongue. No one here right now knows enough about what's going on to pursue that concern yet.

As we are talking, the Flight 93 stragglers start moving through. I tell Chief Chris what we did to help them out in Central City. He nods approval. We agree to keep in touch and set up a communications system of some type soon, even if it's just relay runners. Two small towns in rural Pennsylvania are setting up a loose alliance to help each other. Probably not much different than in the days when George Washington and

Christopher Gist roamed these mountains; you need trustworthy friends to survive.

One of his firefighters escorts us to the roadblock on Hill Road, so we can continue on towards Central City.

Chapter 16 Security, 2015

Some of our trails and fences need some maintenance, as they do every year. I've got a chainsaw, extra gas, bar oil, a come-along, some steel wedges, a shovel and an axe. And it is all loaded on the four-wheeler. I don't have to carry anything! My mom and dad would be rolling over in their grave right now because we brought a four wheeler onto the farmstead.

My parents walked everywhere. Even after four knee replacements, my dad refused to get a four-wheeler. He was still downhill skiing after two knee replacements at the age of seventy-six. He and my mom would cross-country ski. They even tried snowshoeing, but never a snowmobile or four-wheeler to get around, too much noise, too much of a disturbance to nature.

And today we brought in one of those glorified golf carts with fat tires and a lot of room: and a motor. Again, my parents would be horrified! But, we got one hundred and twenty acres of mountain top forest and farm to maintain, with livestock and active farming going on. Rebecca and I are not retired yet; I probably never will retire. So the ability to get around this place fast, and with work gear, beat out Mom and Dad's dislike for four- wheelers. I am sure I will hear them screaming at me from heaven when I finally get a snowmobile!

On the other hand, the security cameras we put in place, Dad would like that. He was not a tech wiz, but being an engineer, he appreciated the value of modern technology. He had a remote sensor put in the driveway twenty years before anything like that even came close to being mainstream. If someone came down the driveway, the doorbell rang. No surprise visitors for Mom and Dad.

***

The security camera system came in to play last Thanksgiving when my brothers and I were talking about what it would take to keep a good eye on the farmstead in an emergency situation. Our fears of a societal or economic collapse had grown. The events following the problematic shootings of black men by police, compounded by the distorted reporting from the media, had led to real unrest in many cities. What if that unrest broke out nationwide?

I said it would take at least nine guys to keep the property secure, three on alert at all times: one at the old farmhouse, main gate, and two patrolling the grounds. My brother John looked at me in disbelief. "Mark," he said, "Get in the twenty-first century, get some trail cams set up! You can get a dozen trail cams with a monitor and control system for a couple thousand bucks. For a bit more you can get cams with low-end night optics. Your biggest expense will be the cabling. I'll help you install it all. With today's technology, it is pretty much plug and go."

As we are talking, I think back to when I bought a cheap trail cam when we lived in the city and busted several people for stealing from my shop because of the pictures it provided. Remote trail cams, it's probably a good idea. A few months later, I took John's advice and bought a remote cam security system. I found a set of six cameras cheap on eBay, really cheap. I bought two sets, with the night optics. I also bought a back-up controller and stuck it and the extra cameras in the Faraday cage.

That summer John and Jan came out for a weekend and we set the system up. We set one cam up in the attic of the old farmhouse looking down the driveway. We set up another looking at the hen house. A third overlooked the cattle pasture, and a fourth looks at where an old logging road comes up from the valley to the corner of the pasture, down where the sweet corn grows. We used almost a thousand feet of cabling for just those four cams. We ran the cable along the fence lines as much as we could, but we had to trench and bury a fair amount of cable, too. I make a mental note to get a couple thousand more feet of cable. Ouch, I think, that will cost as much as the system did.

Now we have trail cams watching the property! They are all wired back to the home office, and I can check on them from my iPhone too! I plan on putting two more out to watch a couple of good hunting spots to see how the deer move. We have the controller set in the home office to start recording when the infrared sensors in the cameras trip. I can remotely change the cameras to operate 24/7. The cabling system has a low voltage line built in to power the cameras. The cams themselves are all stationary, no panning, but we can remote zoom. Overall, it is a very cool system and will allow me to keep a better eye on the property.

Chapter 17 Getting Home, Part 2, September 12, 2018

Hill Road out of Hooversville takes us out of the Stoneycreek River valley and up to the ridge top. I drive the van with most of our crew, Linc drives our newly acquired truck with Ken as shotgun. It is a beautiful road to drive, with many old farmsteads intermixed with gorgeous new homes, built to take advantage of the spectacular views. Today is different. It is still a clear blue sky and the views span for miles. But plumes of heavy smoke rise from many places.

I want to stop and discern the damage. Everyone in the van can see, even here in the remote hills of Pennsylvania, that the devastation is real, and ranges far. The talk from my passengers ranges from bewilderment to rage. I decide we should stop and take in what has happened. It will be tough to do, but we need to face this new reality.

Finding an open stretch of road, with good views to the north and west, and some sightlines to the east, we pull over. I have everyone get out so we can see what is going on. Jerry and Ken stay armed and alert. Britt protests that she just wants to get her kids to the farm, that it is too dangerous to stop. Ken assures her that we need to assess the scene, and that it will be safe. His reassuring words calm her, new respect for him seen in her eyes, even though he is still stone-faced and stern.

Looking out from this vantage point, the scene is incredible. A normally pristine skyline is polluted with plumes of smoke coming from many places. We stare silently at the signs of the distant wreckage and destruction. Conferring with Ken and Jerry, we try to pinpoint the sources. We know of at least three or four large fires in Johnstown, and those plumes, from this distance, make one big dark gray smudge on the western horizon.

There seems to be another large plume coming from what we guess to be the Richland area, but we never saw anything burning up there. The major mall and many shopping plazas are there, and it could be any one of them. A major military presence is there, at the Murtha Airport, and all the National Guard and Army Reserve units based along Airport Road. We hope the military has enough equipment running to fight back the anarchy and fight the fires, too.

Closer, and to the east, is a major forest fire. I state that it must be from the fire I saw yesterday, the coal truck accident by Clear Shade Creek. Another more distant large fire is burning further to the east and again I confirm that it is from the Pleasantville area where I saw the closest plane go down.

As we all look over the wide expanse that we can see from this ridge top, and all the devastation that is taking place before our very eyes, a solemnness overtakes our small group. I ask that we all hold hands and bow our heads, I indicate to Jerry and Ken to join us. God will watch over us as we pray. I quietly ask for God's forgiveness of our sins and that He watch over us and protect us in the dark days ahead. We break hands and turn back to our vehicles, many weeping, knowing what is ahead of us, now that we have seen the devastation before us.

This is rural Pennsylvania. Our biggest town, Johnstown, is on fire. Our major shopping area is on fire. Major parts of the forests are on fire. What must the big cities look like? What is Pittsburgh like, where many of my brothers and sisters live? What about the major cities, Philadelphia, Baltimore, Chicago? New York and Los Angeles were reportedly nuked. Maybe that quick destruction was better than the slow burn that most of the rest of the country will experience. Why has this happened, God? I ask again. The silence is deafening. God always answers our prayers. But not always when we want him to, or in the way we want him to. I know he will answer my prayer, or maybe he already has, I just don't know it yet.

We all load quietly, humbly, into the truck and van. As we drive further down the road, towards the farmstead, we see the big gorgeous homes are still there, but a few are on fire, neighbors futility trying to put them out. The work of the Wagerlys? We do not have the time or the ability to stop and help. We keep a steady course towards Central City.

***

We come in to Central City from the north, Hill Road having eventually run into State Route 160 north of town. We roll up to another makeshift roadblock. Not in town, like earlier, this one has been set up north of town. In the eight hours that we have been gone, someone has gotten smart about the roadblocks. We stop fifty yards short and I step out. "Yo to the roadblock," I holler once again. "We want to pass through to our farm on the other side of town."

"Approach unarmed," I hear in response. I cannot tell who hollered of the several men at the roadblock.

"I am laying down my rifle and side arm, I am your neighbor." I lay down my rifle and pistol. As I walk up to this small group of men, I can see they are tired, agitated and nervous.

As I get close, one of them recognizes me. "Yo, Billy," he says to the apparent leader. "I know'd him, he was talkin' to Reverend Wysinger. He an' his folks got a farm on the other side o' town. Dey be good people, he be all right." I introduce myself to Billy and inquire about where Reverend Wysinger is. He opens the roadblock and he lets us roll through.

A half-mile down the road we come to a large gathering of Flight 93 stragglers, in the parking lot of the Baptist Church. We have seen a couple of farm trucks coming and going down

Main Street and through the roadblock. Those heading north, towards Windber, have been carrying stragglers.

Jerry and I get out of the van. I see Ken get out of the truck and head towards us. Ken nods his head towards St. Paul's Catholic Church across the street, and says he is heading over there for a few minutes, apprehension and relief showing on his face. I nod, and let him know we will wait as long as he needs. Ken was raised Catholic, and he is going to go do what good Catholics do.

I grasp Jerry in a firm handshake, "Jerry, we got you home. Sorry for putting you through so much. You have no idea how glad I was to have you along. I don't even know you, but you are my brother now, don't hesitate to ask for any favors. You helped me save my family from that mess in town, I owe you."

He takes my hand, and pulls me into a big "man hug', with a couple of quick slaps on my back. "You did what I would have done if I had family. I am glad I could help, my brother. I am glad I could help. Keep an eye on Kenny. If he needs someone to talk to, you send him my way. What he did today, not many men have ever done, but I can tell you he is strong, much stronger than he looks. You never know where or when the patriot will stand up. Sometimes it comes from the least expected places. Let him know he is not alone."

I have a tear in my eye as we break apart. "I will do that, my friend, I will do that."

"Tell the Reverend I'll be in tomorrow to talk things over. Let him know everything we saw. He needs to know how bad the situation is. Jerry, you got a good head on your shoulders. You saw how bad it is out there. Help these people get organized for what's coming. God gave you talents and wisdom. Use them to help out this town, to help your neighbors." He nods at me, knowing, and concerned.

Ken comes back from his church, disappointment displayed across his face. He jumps in the van's shotgun seat and silently indicates that we should pull out. I jump in, and wave for Linc to follow. We are far up in the hills, and the few miles to the farmstead should go smoothly.

Fifteen minutes later, as we pull down the long drive to the old farmstead, I hear the big old school bell start to ring as Rusty watches us pull up, a big grin on his face. Becca and Janie come running out, weapons in hand, serious and worried looks across their faces, until they see that it is us.

Chapter 18 Back Home, September 12, 2018

We stop at the big old farmhouse, and Britt is out of the van and hugging Becca before the dust settles under our tires. Larson and Grace are right behind her, and Janie and her boys join in, after coming down off the porch. Linc and Kim step out of the van as well, and take in the surroundings, all that is happening. They smile broadly seeing the farmstead, and the love that is shared here. After the traumatic events of the last two days, this sight is truly peaceful, and welcoming.

I introduce our two newcomers to Becca, and everyone else. Becca steps back and eyes them as a mother hen may look over a new rooster in the hen house, trying to determine friend or foe. Her smile warms genuinely from her instinctive judgment of character. I tell her of how they have no way home, and no family to get to, that they have decided for now, to help us out, and hunker down here.

Talk turns to what we have been through. I tell Blake and Rusty to look after the two youngest boys and little Sarah while the adults talk things over. They protest, wanting to be involved, and both of them are old enough that they should be, but we need them to look after the children. So, with a stern look from their mother, they do as they are told, and sulk back to the farmyard where the three young ones are playing.

We tell Becca and Janie of the roadblocks, the fires, the dead stragglers and the shoot out. We tell them of how things are turning bad in some places, and how people are coming together in other places. How some of the small towns have already been hit by the bandits, and how the townsfolk are pulling together. How some people have turned to chaos, while others are looking for ways to help people out. We talk for over twenty minutes about our trip, what we have seen, and all that has happened. We all agree that anarchy is starting to happen, and that we have to make the farmstead a safe haven. It is also reluctantly agreed upon that we need to help our neighbors, help restore order, and help the stragglers. We all know that we have no plan to do this, but that we must help as much as we can. We end with a short prayer, once again asking God for guidance and wisdom. I think back to my priorities, God first, family second, community third, self last. So how do we help others and not imperil our family? I pray that God will give us the answers.

We all help Ken, Britt and the boys unload, to get moved into the old farmhouse. Linc and Kim will stay in the new house with me and Becca. I let Linc know that I cannot let him be armed in our house. He is a guest in our home, he will be respected and protected. He obliges without any protest, disconcerted about the overall situation, but happy to be somewhere safe.

The talk soon turns to food. Some of us have not eaten in many hours and we have been through exhaustive ordeals. Becca and Janie tell us they have already started a large pot of bean and ground beef chili. We can all eat within an hour or so. I tell Linc that he will keep watch on the front porch with me while everyone else gets settled in, and gets something to eat. His wife, Kim, volunteers to bring our dinner out to us when it's ready.

Linc and I settle in on the front porch. I grab a bottle of cheap bourbon, and pour us each two fingers, neat. I silently offer him a glass as I eye him over, head to toe. He is well dressed, in a practical sense, good hiking boots, not dress shoes, Levi jeans, not designer jeans, lightweight, but sturdy two-pocket shirt over a tee shirt. He also has an over-the-shoulder pack with him. I realize that what he is wearing is all he has in the world. His car is dead, at the Flight 93 Memorial. What he packed for the trip is in a hotel room in Johnstown.

His home is five hundred miles away and might as well be on the far side of the moon. And despite this, he is remarkably calm, composed.

"You're an engineer, you're a smart guy, what do you think happened, Linc?" I ask.

He sighs. He looks at his feet for a few moments, then looks back up at the sky, and the fading light in the east. Not a contrail to be seen, only a few ugly gray smudges of smoke on the horizon. A redwinged blackbird skirts down the fence line, and a few goldfinches peck at the sunflower seed in the feeder. The goldenrod sway in the evening breeze, the nearby oak leaves rustle. A bright red cardinal chirps as he and his mate cautiously make their way to the seed scattered below the feeder.

"Mark, this is surreal. I don't believe what I have seen with my own eyes. When this all started yesterday, I thought, as you did, an EMP. Because of my work in shale fracking, I've looked at how a massive power outage would affect oil and gas production. What I found out scared me. That is why I started my own simple preparations back home, a few guns, extra ammunition, an overstocked pantry, stuff like that. I knew transportation and manufacturing would grind to a halt, as well as food delivery. But I never imagined that societal chaos would erupt so fast!

"When I realized what happened, while we were at the Memorial ceremony, I thought Kim and I had a shot at getting back home, especially after seeing the aid station in Central City. But after seeing what is going on in Johnstown! That blew me away. Then the drug freaks on the road here! This is Bible belt territory, and it's anarchy. I can't imagine what's going on in the bigger cities.

"You all have guns to defend yourselves. And, out here in the country, you at least have the possibility of providing for yourselves. In the cities, where food will start to run out in another day or so, the biggest and the strongest will just take from the weaker and the helpless. It won't be long until everyone in the cities start to move out towards the country, looking for food. I never really thought this through, it's bad, real bad." He looks back down at his feet and shakes his head again. He looks back up, and the stress on his face is evident, tears starting to well in his eyes. He wipes his face and eyes with his shirtsleeve, not wanting to show his distress, trying to be the strong man we all want to be.

The sky has turned a deep blue. Wispy strands of reds and pinks fade to the darker oranges and purples of a beautiful sunset. We sit in silence for several minutes, sipping the cheap bourbon. The cardinal pair comes into the feeder for a last bit of sunflower seed as the light continues to fade.

"I never figured on this either, my friend, didn't think it would be an EMP. Figured economic collapse, maybe social or political revolt of some sort. The dependent class getting tired of handouts, or the working class getting tired of just getting by. Look at the last election. That was a revolt against the Washington establishment, and the crony capitalism that has wrecked this country. People got tired of the regulations and tax codes that have fed the DC fat cats and Wall Street insiders while middle America slowly crumbled.

"But on the other hand, an EMP doesn't surprise me. America has become weak, no longer respected. Both the Iranians and the North Koreans have wanted to bring the Western world to its knees. Radical Islam has wanted to do the same for centuries. Or maybe the crazy Russian dictator pulled the trigger, or the Pakistanis. Really, it doesn't matter who did it. We retaliated by now, that's for sure, all those nuke subs we got. You can be sure that what we are experiencing here is going on there, too. I'm kind of surprised we haven't seen ground level nukes going off, too. We would all be fried then, not just the grid.

"But we are prepared here, Linc, we will live through this. I always figured, as a Christian, my duty is to help others. We have always done that. But I always figured that if things went bad, we needed to be prepared, able to take care of our own first. Only then could we be in a position to help others. How would we be able to help other people if we could not take care of ourselves? So for the last five years or so, we have been getting ready, getting this place ready, for something like this."

"I can see that," Linc responds. "You have a lot going on here, more than just solar power and vegetable gardens, not to mention some chickens and a few pigs."

"You have a sharp eye, and a keen mind, Linc," I respond. "I'm starting to like you." We chuckle a bit together. "And you stepping out, helping to protect our caravan, that helped out, too. You stepped out to help protect my family. I respect that.

"Let me tell you how I think this is going to play out, Linc. We're already into day two. Those who have not figured it out, those who think the government is going to fix it, most of them are a lost cause, they are going to starve or get killed. That's harsh, I know, but it's the truth. Fifty million people depend on the government to feed and house them. They have no clue about self-reliance, and will be lost. Within the next seven days, only the smart and the strong will survive. That's sad to say. Within two weeks everyone will start to get desperate for food. The smart will have stored food or figured out how to get food. The strong will just take the food from the weak. But that will start to run out, too. Sickness will be a big problem as well. The water will start to go bad, dysentery, cholera and other diseases will run rampant. I hate to say it, but millions will die from diseases long thought vanquished.

"Then those still strong enough or smart enough will start to move out in search of food. They will start to move towards the country where there are farms; cows, pigs, corn, potatoes. But what they don't realize is that without power, even the farms will start to shut down. How will a dairy operation work without the mechanized milkers? How will a chicken farm work without the mechanized feeders, the regular delivery of feed? Even the farm industry will collapse without power. Unmilked cows dry up, unfed chickens don't produce eggs and will die, crops not harvested feed no one, crops not being able to be sent to market rot.

"Farmers will start looking to recruit laborers to help them run the farms, and the smart people will join up with them. But the thugs, they will just try to take what they need. That is where the conflict will arise. Between those willing to work to keep things going, and those who will just want to take what they need to survive. We saw the beginning of that today, with those Wagerly boys.

"That's were you come in, Linc. I think you and Kim fall in the smart people category. Are you willing to pitch in and work? Willing to help out those who need it, who deserve it? I think you know you are going to have to use your smarts to help us all survive. We need your help, I hope I read you well."

Rebecca and Kim have returned to the front porch with chili and corn bread for us. They have stood silently by, as Linc and I discussed the situation. Becca says slowly, compassionately, "Mark, that is a very grim outlook. Do you really think that is what lies ahead? I know we have talked about this, but will it really get that bad?"

Kim sets the bowls of chili down before us and turns to Becca. She says sullenly, "You would not believe what we saw out there today, massive fires, people shot dead on the side of the road, roadblocks. Becca, I barely know you, but what your

146

husband is saying, we have seen it. And I'll speak for me and my husband. Our home is five hundred miles away, we wouldn't make it thirty miles in the chaos we have seen. If you need help here, we will help you. I totally understand what your husband is saying. We have nothing but the clothes we are wearing, yet you have offered us help. For that you have our gratitude and loyalty. We aren't used to such rugged spirituality, but I do believe we all need God on our side. Linc and I will gladly take you up on your offer to stay here, and we will gladly help out as you may need. Hopefully, eventually, things will settle down, and we can make it home..." She begins to sob lightly, "Oh my God, I can't believe what has happened! I can't believe I may be stuck here in these mountains." She begins to weep heavily and clings to her husband. "Oh my God, Linc, oh my God, what has happened? Has this really happened?" She breaks down in tears, clinging to her husband, sobbing, the reality of the day finally hitting home, the desperation of their situation fully coming to light.

We sit silently together. With a few loving words from her husband, Kim begins to regain her composure. I ask that we all hold hands as Becca and I recite our normal family grace before Linc and I have our meal. We both start to eat tentatively, but after a few spoonfuls, we realize how hungry we are, after all we have been through. Our bowls of chili and the plate of corn bread are finished off quickly. Becca goes back to replenish them as Kim and Linc quietly console each other.

***

My mind is so full of things that need to be done. There are all the daily farm chores to do, and now we have to deal with chaos setting in around us. We need to determine what systems have survived and what needs to be replaced. The security system and cameras are down, that needs to be evaluated, and brought back on line. How intact are the solar and wind systems? What about the battery bank and inverter system? That all needs to be checked over. We know it works, but are there any problems we don't know about? What about the mundane things? Has anyone fed the animals this evening? Are the chickens locked in their coop?

I hear Larson talking with his mom in the living room, and I holler through the screen door for him to have his mom and dad, Grace, Janie, Rusty and Blake come out on to the porch with us.

Darkness has finally settled across our mountain retreat. Not a light can be seen anywhere. The blinking lights from the nearby windmills are off. No lights from the radio towers in the distance. No faint glow from nearby communities. Only the moon and the stars, and they seem brighter than ever with no manmade light to fade their glory.

After Becca has returned with more chili for me and Linc, all the adults and mature children are now on the front porch of the old farmhouse. I size up our group, seven adults and four teenagers, eleven in all, with three youngsters that need looking after. I ask Janie about her young ones and she says they are settled down and should be all right, that she can stick around to hear what's going on.

"It's getting late and we need to get some order here," I begin, my commander's voice kicks in from the few years I spent in the military, no discussion here, just state what's going to happen. "Y'all know that the grid is down. Bad things are happening in the world. You have seen it. And we can't let those bad things happen here. So we have to keep security up here, like Rusty and Blake did today, right boys." I say.

"Yeah, Pap, we got it. Holler at strangers to stop and keep armed and alert," says Rusty.

"What about the bell?" I ask.

"Ring it loud and long, and shoot at anyone who doesn't listen to us," chimes in Blake.

"Good. Y'all hear that? We can't let anyone in here that we don't know. And we have to keep guard on the front gate all night, starting tonight, okay? Here is how it's going to work tonight. Becca, you, Britt, Rusty and Blake, you all make sure the farm chores are done tonight, and tomorrow morning, and make us all a good breakfast, too. Janie, you look after your young'uns. Linc and I will stay put on the front porch till 2:00. Ken, we'll wake you then. You and Larson will watch till sun up. Kim, you go with Becca, get settled in, and help her out any way you can. That will get us through the night, but we will need a regular shift set up. Ken, can you work on setting up a shift roster for us?" He nods his consent, still grim faced, a little tired looking around his eyes.

"I can't tell you all how thankful I am that we got everyone here. I wish Zach was here too, hopefully he will be soon. But he is safe where he is. You all are tired, I'm sure, but there gotta be questions? Have I forgotten anything?"

There is quiet for a few moments. Then Becca speaks up quietly, but with sincerity. "We need to pray, Mark. God will hear us, we need to pray." She is quiet for a few moments. "Dear God, have mercy on our family. As you have brought terrible times upon this world for turning against you, know that we still hold you dear. We love you for all you have provided us. We know, by your grace, that we are redeemed. Help us to be strong in our faith. May your hand of protection be upon us, and this farmstead. Help us to be a beacon to those in need. Grant us wisdom to make it through these trying times. Dear Lord, please continue to give us strength to proclaim you greatness. In Christ's name we do pray, Amen." Hands are squeezed and "Amen" is quietly repeated.

Hugs are shared around as the unity in Christ is felt. Talk begins to divert and shifts to who sleeps where, who feeds the chickens, who puts out hay, which kid gets a flash light. A bit of normalcy is setting in. Becca takes charge, and gets everyone moving.

Ken is standing off to the side of the porch, stoic. He responds to his kids' and wife's questions almost robotically, with no emotion. After most people have headed off the porch, I walk over, and stand beside him quietly. We both gaze over the darkness in front of us.

"I don't know what to say, Ken. What you did today, not many men can do, would do."

He nods, silently, not taking his eyes off the country lane leading into the farmstead. He still has the scoped 30.06 gripped firmly in his hands.

"Did you eat?" I ask.

"A little."

"What happened at your church?"

"The priest was dead, shot through the head. Killed himself. Pistol was next to his hand."

"Oh shit. Ken, I am so sorry, you looked for help, oh shit, I am so sorry."

"Screw the church. God is God, he don't need no church. I don't need no church. What I did, I had to do. I'm okay, Mark."

We stand quietly together for several minutes. I struggle, trying to find the right words to help my son-in-law deal with what has happened. Struggling to deal with what has happened myself. My faith gives me resolution. I find the words I hope will help Ken.

"What you did today, Ken, by the bridge, that was an act of bravery, that took strength and courage. You stood up against evil. What the priest did, that was cowardice. You had the conviction that you have a life to live, more to give for our Lord, for your family. The priest did not have faith that he had more to give. You are a stronger man, Ken. You made a tough decision to protect your family. He was weak. You showed your strength, Ken. You did what needed to be done. God's grace and love knows that your actions were justified."

Ken nods, as he stares into the darkness. After a few minutes of silence, he turns and gives me a warm hug. He wordlessly heads into the old farmhouse, and hopefully some sleep before his watch comes.

I walk back to where Linc sits silently, looking into the darkness that is our front drive. A bit of moonlight allows us to see the dim outline of the nearby trees, and more distant cornfield. The cut in the line of tall corn where our lane comes through is very distinguishable, even in the darkness. We hear cackling and squawking as the chickens and ducks are fed, shortly followed by the grunts of pigs, and low mooing of our four steers, happy to be fed, even if it's late.

Linc and I sit quietly. The stars are brilliant, the Milky Way clearly painting a dim swath across the night sky. We talk a bit of our pasts, a bit about the future. But mainly we are both consumed by our own thoughts of the past two days and what lies ahead. The night passes along, and we wake Ken and Larson to replace our guard. I am very glad to see that Ken was sleeping. I guide Linc to the new house, and his new bedroom. Then I disrobe, and crawl into bed with my wife. She snuggles against me, the warmth of her skin against mine comforts me.

Chapter 19 Moxham, Day 2, Herc's Story, September 12, 2018

Herc wakes next to his soul mate, Leesa, after a fitful night's sleep. Her body fits well with his. Despite the troubles of the day before, they enjoy their love for each other. Herc's ebony skin glistens with sweat, even though the morning air is cool. His muscles are tight, but he feels the tension release from his body. He had walked almost ten miles to get home the day before. He is glad that he is home with his wife and child.

He was on the jobsite the day before when everything stopped. The power went out; the power tools quit working, cars and trucks wouldn't run, cell phones were dead. After a few hours of waiting for things to come back on, he and the crew cleaned up, packed up and he started walking home.

He got home at dusk. By this time he knew something bad had happened. Stalled cars everywhere, no power anywhere. Some people were starting to freak out. He was carrying his side arm, as always, and had no fear coming into Moxham, not the best of neighborhoods. He could see a bad fire had burned down a few buildings and some people were starting to panic. He saw fights breaking out in the parking lot of a Dollar General and watched as looters took over the store.

Herc has never had fear, at least not from physical violence. He is a well-built man. Not tall, but very muscular. Fifteen years in the construction trade has kept him fit. He is a gentle and loving man, hard working and independent. But his intolerance to racist comments or insults to family and friends has put him in a few brawls. He knows how to take care of himself.

As the dawn comes to full light, his senses are heightened, he can tell something is wrong. More wrong than the power being out. There is a tension in the air, distant sounds and foul smells. Something is not right. He urges Leesa to take care of their child as he heads outside

The distinct acrid smell of burning vinyl siding is heavy in the air. A thick dark plume of smoke can be seen through the trees. The plume is big, and not far away. He heads back in and tells Leesa to pack up clothes fast, there's a big fire close by. He grabs weapons and ammunition. Five minutes later, with his girl and child, they head several blocks away, to his mom's house. Other people are doing the same, packing up what they can and heading away from the fire. More panic today than he saw yesterday. He keeps his family close, and hurries deliberately to his mom's house, away from the fire.

His mom and stepdad are happy to see them, but are also concerned about the fire. The plume of smoke shows this fire is big. And no sirens, no firetrucks; what can stop this inferno? A fire the day before burned out after destroying an entire block. This fire looks bigger.

Herc tells his family he is going to walk down the street and see what's happening. People are flooding away from the fire, but a few are heading towards it. Some are curious, they want to see the devastation, some are like Herc, they want to see if they can stop it, if they can help. He meets up with several friends and acquaintances as he heads towards the billowing smoke.

A block away from the inferno, they can see that the fire is massive. People are no longer scurrying past with some possessions, people are running with what they have on their backs, some are pleading for help for trapped loved ones. The scene is surreal. Flames lick into the air, fifty feet above the homes. The smoke is thick, boiling black and gray. The old maples and elms spanning the street, are ablaze, allowing the fire to spread from street to street. This fire will spread across the entire neighborhood. One of Herc's friends says they need to get ahead of the fire, and start cutting down the trees, cut a firebreak. Herc has a chain saw, so does one of his friends. A guy listening in, says there's a backhoe in his neighbor's yard, who was having some sewer work done. They can use that to pull the trees away. They come up with a plan to cut a firebreak two blocks up; one block higher than Herc's house. But it's gotta get done.

They begin the task of cutting down the large trees that span the roads, trees with twenty- four inch trunks rising fifty feet tall. Some fall on cars or get hung up on other trees. Some take out power lines and utility poles. More people join in to help, mainly to pull the felled trees away. Houses and other property are damaged in the effort. Some men from the fire department walk in with hoses and chain saws, and start to help out.

They spend the next four chaotic hours cutting and moving trees. The fire is contained, if a hundred houses burning to the ground can be considered contained. Herc did not even see his own home burn down, too busy trying to save his neighbors' homes.

***

Herc is back at his Mom's house that afternoon, trying to assess the situation, trying to figure out what they need to do to survive. He has heard gunshots, and has heard that some of the drug dealers are causing problems, as well as the drug addicts looking to take advantage of the situation, to rob and steal to support their habit. Herc is armed and alert, watching over his family.

With the power out, the freezer is off. Good meat will go to waste so Herc's mom decides to grill some steaks in the backyard. Better to eat it than lose it. Herc is in the house when he hears a commotion outside. He doesn't think much of it at first as there has been a lot of commotion all day. Then he hears two guns shots, close, not far away like before. He jumps from the couch, and races outside. Before he even opens the back door he hears several more gunshots, loud, in his back yard.

Gun drawn, he steps around the doorway to see his mom lying on the ground next to the grill, bleeding. His stepdad lays motionless on the steps. His brother's eyes are glazing over as his 12 gauge pump drops from his hands. He sees one guy, motionless on the street, and two more guys going after the food on the grill. Without thinking, without saying a word, he shoots both gangsters from twenty feet away. Double squeeze, center mass. A few thousand rounds down range make the motion automatic.

Leesa is screaming behind him, as is John Jr. Herc is in a rage. His momma is dead. He races to the street, and sees two people he knows are drug punks running away, turning the corner onto Cypress Street. His adrenaline kicks in, and he chases after them, turning the corner only ten yards behind them. He unloads the last dozen rounds left in his clip, and both thugs fall to the ground.

He runs up on them, rage boiling as he envisions his mom's lifeless body lying in the yard. He kicks the dead body heavily in the side, screaming at the lifeless form for being so stupid. The other would-be meat thief groans, attracting Herc's attention. He turns and kicks him in his bloody gut. "You stupid son of a bitch! You killed my momma for some food!" He screams at the prone young man. "She'd a given you food, you dumb ass! You stupid son of a bitch!" Herc kicks him even harder several times in the body and head. The groaning stops, completely. A crowd has gathered by this time, mostly known neighbors, but a few strangers too, unfriendly faces.

Herc turns to them all. Realization of what he has just done, what has just happened, starting to sink in. He drops to his knees and starts to cry. "They killed my momma," he exclaims. His emotions turn hard again. "No one messes with me and mine without paying a price. Y'all stay away from me and mine! Ya hear! Don't mess with me!" He starts sobbing again. Leesa has come up to him at this point, and starts to lead him back to the house. Many follow to comfort him, some slink away to report what they have seen.

Chapter 20 Wagerly's Compound, Day 2, September 12, 2018

He rolls over and checks the alarm clock as the sun seeps in around the pulled down curtains. The clock is blank. He smiles, the electricity is still out. His head is pounding slightly from the wine he drank the night before. "Which chick is it that likes the wine?" he asks out loud, "I got to get rid of her, I don't get no headaches from whiskey." He looks over at the two female forms in the bed next to him. He gives a strong kick to the closest one. "Which of you two bitches had me drinkin' wine! Get out! It don't matter, the powers still out, and I got things to do." He lets off in a string of curses as he chases the two women from his room. He needs some time to think. This is the opportunity of a lifetime.

Frank Wagerly is a hard man who has spent time in jail. He has a leadership quality that other men and women of bad character will follow. He is mean, but decisive, smart and commanding. He doesn't do the drugs he sells. He had tried the meth that he and his boys made, but realized how poisonous it was. But that didn't stop him from making and selling it. More recently he had gotten into the opiate trade, everything from over the counter drugs to heroin. He quickly realized that an opioid-addicted man would soon become a heroin addict, and a constant stream of cash to him and his crew.

Frank had felt something like this power outage would happen; and now is his chance to become a king. He knows he needs to act now, to inflict terror, and establish himself as the top dog in the violent world that he will help create.

When the power had not come back on by sunset the day before, he sent a crew to Hooversville, and they had come back with booze from the bars and drugs from the pharmacy. He had sent another group out to loot people on Route 30, and grab what women they could find. His small group of about twenty people in his compound had already grown to thirty. As he is splashing water on his face to wipe away some of the grime, he hears a few more bikes and a truck come rumbling in. Today is going to be a good day.

The newly arrived group tells of power out everywhere, of panic, and looting, fires burning, and no one responding. People are starting to walk the streets, trying to get home, looking for family or just looking for food and water. Frank licks his lips, and smiles at the news of chaos starting.

He had noticed that the helicopter flights in and out of Flight 93 had stopped, so he knew the army was done in the area. Those people at the Memorial were now his cattle, no one was coming to help them. He needs to send out raiders to shut down anyone on the roads. He needs to make sure the local roads get shut down so he can raid the farms freely. That will leave people confined to the few small towns and unable to communicate with each other. Then he can dominate the area, controlling the roads and controlling the farms, then controlling the towns.

He has the most firepower, the most people, and he will be ruthless. He will control the area then expand from there. Maybe go down to Somerset and bust out his friends at the state prison, then move on and take control of the whole two counties. He thinks of Johnstown, but dismisses it. If he can control the countryside he would control the food, then he could command anything he wanted from the city folk, even the gang bangers.

He doesn't expect much opposition to his grand scheme. Maybe a farmer and his boys with a couple of hunting rifles making a stand someplace. But he has mean and hardened people who want drugs and booze. So long as he has drugs and booze to feed them, they will do his bidding.

They have four working trucks, several working bikes, a few quads, and an old Ford Torino. They need to get out and start implementing his vision of terror. He stumbles to the main living area of his compound. Some people are up and moving while others are curled up in blankets or sleeping bags. A bright-eyed skinny girl is making coffee in a percolator. She is scratching at her tiny arms as she puffs on a cigarette.

Frank starts rousting the motley crew from their booze and drug-induced haze. His haphazard crew gets coffee and food. Some get a fix, some get a drink. There are cheers about the successful raid on the Hooversville bars and pharmacy. Frank hears about the gunfire and that some townsfolk got killed. Outwardly he boasts that the cowards will now cower at their approach. But he has a nagging feeling that they may have wakened a sleeping dog, that the next time they approach the town, it won't be so easy.

He sends out three groups. One of bikers that are to run the back roads, keep people from roaming, from talking to each other. One is to run along Route 30 and past Flight 93 again; kill anyone they want, there is no law. Take anything of value. Keep people off the roads. If you find a woman you like, have her, bring her back if you want, but only if she will be useful. He sends another truck to do the same on the smaller state routes. They'll have the whole area bottled up before the locals even know what's happened.

By late morning word gets back to Frank that they killed a lot of people on Route 30, people who were at the Memorial ceremony. What's left of those folk are terrified and bottled up on the Memorial grounds. Meanwhile a few more people have arrived by bike, old trucks, and a couple vintage cars. A few are bikers that have been to his compound before. They came all the way from Pittsburgh, not druggy types, but hard core convicts, organized bike gang members. They tell him more are on the way, as soon as they can get their bikes running and a convoy organized. The scenes they describe, from the outskirts of Pittsburgh, are joy to his ears. Rioting, looting, shops burning. Cops are unable to respond, and those that do are being shot. They tell of a few areas where the locals have banded together to form posses, roadblocks, but mayhem and anarchy seem to have set in.

By mid-afternoon, the Route 30 truck has come back, and a new crew has been sent out, same with the biker crew that was roaming the back roads. But nothing has been heard from the other truck that was on the smaller state roads. That truck had two of his sons with them. As a few more hours tick by he gets furious that they have not returned. Finally, late that day, word gets back to him. One of his users gets out of Hooversville, and reports to him that some vigilante types had ambushed his boys on Route 403. They had killed them all in cold blood. All but one, and that was his nephew. He got executed in town, the addict tells him. The addict spins a story, making Frank's boys out to be heroes, and describes the ambushers in detail, what they were driving, what they looked like, where they were heading. The addict is expecting a reward for his courage in coming there, a fix to his addiction. The fix is fast and permanent as Frank puts a bullet through his head.

"I want these sons-a-bitches dead! Not now, not tomorrow, yesterday! You let these townsfolk know, this man, and his family of Jesus-loving religious bastards, this vigilante group, they killed my boys. They are dead. We will find them, and we will kill them, all of them!"

A few men nudge at a larger man, who has been leading the bikers on the back roads. He speaks up. "Frank, the towns are setting up roadblocks."

Frank blows up. "Country pipsqueaks putting out a few barriers! Hairy, you tellin' me you can't run a roadblock set up by some local yocals? Get out there and give them some terror.

You scared of a few fat old men and a couple of pimply-faced teenagers behind a few lawn chairs! Don't give me this shit, Hairy, we are going to own those towns! You get out there, and tell me what we need to run over these backwards Bible thumpers. We got the fire power, we'll use it if we need to."

"I left a couple guys to watch 'em, Frank. They're moving cars and trucks into the roadblocks. One of my guys says there's someone stops by every now and then, and gives them directions. Each time this guy stops by, he sees new stuff going on, better placement of cars and people, better rotation of folks. It ain't no fat men with shotguns, they're getting serious, Frank. Shooting up their town last night got them moving."

"We can take care of that, we'll blow those roadblocks up!" Frank replies vehemently. "Now let's get some defense set up here, in case these bastards get ambitious." He goes off on a cussing tirade that puts people in gear getting a defense set up. He heads back to the main camp, slaps the closest woman and grabs her by the arm. He heads back to his private lair.

Chapter 21   Moxham, Night 2, Herc's Story, September 12, 2018

Leesa gets Herc back to his mom's house. His mom, brother and stepdad are dead. He and two close friends console each other as they dig three graves in his backyard, Herc knows there will be no coroner, no police investigation, no mortician.

He is a religious man, but he does not have the words. He bows his head with Leesa, John Jr., and a larger gathering of friends, who have heard what happened. "God loves you, Momma. I know you are with him now." He starts to sob, but he cannot continue. One of Herc's aunts speaks up, and continues a prayer for the deceased. Once again, it is all too surreal, a backyard burial, as people stream by in distress. The neighborhood is falling apart around them, as they honor three lives cut short by violence.

Just as the funeral gathering begins to somberly break up, a semi-druggie friend rushes up and grabs Herc by the arm. "Dude, you gotta git outta here. Big Paulie has it in for you. One of those dudes you gunned down was his brother. They're gonna come for ya." In broken sentences, he tells Herc what he's heard.

The guy is a social security drug addict dependent who Herc has done a few favors for. Herc finds out that Big Paulie, a New Jersey import and major drug dealer, has declared Moxham his turf, and sent out his soldiers to claim what they wanted. Herc was the first to stand against him, and now he is pissed that someone would fight back. He is even more pissed that his brother got killed. The dependent drug addict tells Herc that he heard Big Paulie was sending a crew out to get him that night.

"Yeah, that ain't gonna happen." Herc responds darkly.

After the informant leaves, Herc checks over his arsenal. He arms several of his neighbors as needed. Several other neighbors already have long guns and side arms. Herc is not a strategist nor a strong leader, but some plan is better than no plan. "If those assholes roll up here you clock 'em. Okay?" is all the direction anyone gets. They all nod.

As dusk turns to darkness, an uncle and nephew state they are going to stay there. Their home has burned down, they have nowhere to go and they can help keep a watch out. Herc accepts their help with a big smile, and hugs all around. They set up a loose shift schedule to sit on the back porch and keep an eye out.

***

A bit after midnight Big Paulie, and part of his Jersey crew walks up the street, four of them, and Big Paulie. Two semi-automatic weapons, a sawed-off shogun, and four side arms. Herc and all of his neighbors are awakened by the boom of the 9mm that kills Herc's dozing cousin. Herc rolls out of a light sleep, and grabs his 30/30 lever action with a powerful Mag-light that he had strapped on earlier that night. As he steps to the second floor window he snaps on the powerful light, and immediately blinds the ambushers. His first shot puts down the guy that shot his cousin. He starts shooting at other targets in the street, the other would-be ambushers. His uncle opens up from the front porch with the 12 gauge pump. Three of the ambushers manage to duck behind the cover of cars and neighbors' houses. Random shots are fired in his direction. Many come straight through the window Herc is shooting from. He feels the sting as a bullet creases his shoulder. Dropping to the ground, he realizes his powerful light that at first helped him, now is drawing fire. He clicks it off, and moves to the next bedroom, to find a new firing position.

The gunfire springs his neighbors into action. Within minutes, gunfire from all directions is coming down on the three remaining New Jersey hoodlums trapped on the street. Two more street thugs end up dead. Big Paulie manages to drag himself off the street and heads back to his lair.

As the shooting dies down, shouts ring out. Herc's neighbors and friends are hollering to figure out if any thugs are still out there, if any of their friends need help. A few minutes later the neighbors meet in the street. Herc is on his porch and beckons them all over. "You don't want to be on the street like that, all in a big group. That ain't good." He chides them. "We all gotta be smart. This shit is gonna get worse. They'll be back, and ya'll be dead unless ya'll get organized and fight back." He leaves them standing in his yard as he goes into his momma's house to calm a stoic Leesa.

***

"We ain't stayin here, Herc," Leesa states.

"Ain't nowhere to go," says Herc.

'Ain't nowhere to stay either, genius! That bastard, Paulie, I know'd him, before I met you, I used to go with his brother, the one you killed tonight. We can't stay here, he came here heavy, we got lucky, we gotta go. He'll come back, and he'll burn us out. I know'd them, Herc, they is meaner than a rattlesnake!"

Moxham had never been kind to Herc. He had tried to make it his home but he has constantly been confronted with drug addicts, bigoted cops, and other troubles. His home of five years has burned down, his momma and brother are dead. He has many cousins, uncles and aunts in the area, but with the new troubles now, he instinctively knows he needs to leave. The question is how? And where to?

Chapter 22 3rd Morning, Farmstead, September 13, 2018

The sun rises about 6:30 in early fall in the mountains of western Pennsylvania. Which means the critters and birds and other mountain noises let you know the day has started at about 5:30. But we get awaken before all that by the front porch bell ringing loudly.

The distinctive clanging wakes both me and Becca instantly. "Oh crap," I say as I leap out of bed, pulling on a pair of old shorts and a sweatshirt. My mind races. It has to be stragglers, can't be bandits, not yet. I would have heard shots by now if it were bandits. Ken would have let loose on anyone threatening us. But the bell continues to clang. I need to get to the old farmhouse asap! "Becca, something's happening. Get up, be alert, wake up Linc and Kim. I'm heading up to the front gate." She looks a little panicked, but throws on a pair of jeans and a shirt.

"I'm coming with you," she says. "The kids are up there, I'm coming with you."

I grab her by the shoulders, firmly but not hard. "You need to stay here. If there is a problem, this is where we'll come. I think it's just stragglers. No shots have been fired. Ken is up there, he won't let anything bad happen to the kids, Okay?" She calms down a bit, and nods her approval.

I grab my AR15, check the load and stick two spare clips in my shorts pocket as I head out the door. I've got to make a standard load vest, I think, as I start up the short lane to the farmhouse. The bell ringing has slowed to a once every fifteen seconds clang, and I can hear some loud back and fourth conversation that does not sound threatening. I come around the side of the old farmhouse, gun at half ready, and eye up the situation.

Ken is on the porch, kneeling behind the railing, 30.06 tight to his shoulder. He is calmly telling a guy in an old farm truck to stand with his hands up next to his truck, and to wait. Larson rings the bell once more. I glance at the house, and see Janie standing in the doorway with an AR15.

"Stand down everyone," I yell. "Stand down. It's all good! That's Thad our neighboring farmer. It's all good."

"Mark, Mark, am I glad to see you!" Thad exclaims as he runs towards us. "I got problems, and I need your help." He is panting as I meet him on the old lane.

"My milker is down! Well, the generator that runs the milker is down. Things were tight last month and I didn't refill my spare gas cans. The generator ran out of gas. We finished off last night's milking by hand, but we need to get my generator running or that milk will go sour and those cows will go dry. I don't want to be intruding, but I need some gas. You got to help me out, buddy, I'm against the wall here. Can you help me out?"

"Larson," I holler, "Get on up here. We need your help." Larson scurries up. I have him take Thad's two five gallon cans back to our gas pump by the old barn and fill them up.

"We can fill up those two cans, Thad, which may last you a few days, but we need a long term solution. Did you get to town and pick up your wife the other day?"

"Sure did, Mark," Thad replies. "We brought Momma home cause things were so bad at the home. But I don't think we can take care of Momma. She needs meds, and oxygen that we don't have. Terri's all torn up about it. I told her what you said about us being attacked. She don't believe it. Now we can't even milk the cows. Crap, Mark, shit's gone to hell! But you are right, brother, we need a plan, or I'm gonna lose some cows."

"These cans will get you through for a bit, Thad. And there are abandoned cars and trucks out there that you can siphon off. You got to keep that dairy herd going, Thad. Those cows are more important than you know. I'm gonna want to get a few of them cows from you, to mate with my bulls. We got to keep the herd going, the old fashioned way. So we'll do what we can to help you out."

"I appreciate the gas for the generator," says Thad, shaking my hand. "I think things will come back around to normal real quick tho', buddy, but if you need a couple of cows, maybe we can work something out." Larson returns, lugging the two five gallon cans, and we load them in Thad's old truck. With a thank you, he heads off down the drive to the main road, no more than a neighbor helping a neighbor in his mind. I hope he starts to realize that it's more than that now.

***

I look to the east, with Larson at my side. The slight glow of the sunrise is turning the sky to various shades of pinks, yellows, purples and oranges.

"What do you see there, Larson?" I ask, as we both gaze at the splendid colors vividly spreading before us.

"Sunrise, Pap, A new day," Larson replies.

"You are exactly right, my young friend. And look at how beautiful it is. God is still with us, he would not give us such a beautiful sight, such encouragement. Larson, we have a lot to do, let's get to doing it, okay?"

Larson looks at me a little sideways, like he thinks I may be a crazy old man. But there is also respect in the sideways glance, like maybe he thinks I know what I'm doing. I hope I know what I'm doing.

With the noise of the clanging bell, the rushing about, and all the other commotion, the whole compound is starting to stir. It's country wake-up time by now anyways, animals need fed! The chicken and ducks are starting to show a bit of attitude, expecting food. The pigs and beaf cows are starting to mill around their feed troughs, expecting something good.

I head to the old farmhouse, and see Rusty and Blake, semi-dressed, semi-awake. They have both been here on long weekends, and overnights in summers past. They both know what needs to be done on a normal country morning. "Y'all got some chores to do! Them animals won't shut up till you feed 'em. Y'all get at it, okay?"

They nod at me, a little bleary eyed. Blake looks back, and asks if they should take their guns with them. Wow, I think, the thirteen year old already gets it. "I don't remember giving you a gun to carry around, Blake," I say.

"No, Pap, you didn't, but with all we heard about, don't ya think we ought to have a gun with us, in case something else bad happens?"

"Yeah, Pap, what if one of the bandits comes up on us while we're feeding the pigs and cows. We need to be prepared," Rusty adds. He was armed with a 12 guage shotgun the day bedore. At fifteen, he has been trained with most of or hunting weapons. Blake has been trained too, but only with the smaller caliber weapons

I can't argue with their statement, and getting these teenagers used to being armed, considering what I think may be ahead... "Okay, guys, follow me back to the new house," I say.

Back at the house, I give Rusty a 12 gauge pump, making sure he knows the mechanics and reload procedure. Blake gets a 22 caliber squirrel gun, again only after he has shown he knows the rifle.

"Keep the guns no more than an arm's length away. Stay alert, okay?"

"We'll be okay, Pap. We just want to be ready if some bad people show up. We'll be cool, Pap," says Rusty. "And I'll keep an eye on Blake, Pap, okay?"

"Yeah, Rusty, you do that. And, Blake, no horsing around out there. You get them animals fed and then come back in for breakfast. And no pot shots with those guns, no target practice at tin cans. If we hear shootin', we'll think it's trouble. Now get goin'."

They head out to the barn to feed the animals. Young teenagers, armed and loaded, is this the new normal?

Breakfast is a little subdued. Even with Kim and Linc on guard at the old farmhouse, it's still a large group of people who don't normally eat breakfast together. After a traumatic couple of days, people are keeping their thoughts to themselves. Janie is the most active, trying to feed the three young ones, and keep them settled. Becca takes charge of little Sarah, easing Janie's load considerably.

Britt and Larson start clearing the table, Ken somberly starts helping to clean up, too.

"What's going to happen today, Pap?" Grace asks me.

"That's a good question, youngun. First, I think we need to have your momma and Grammy take a look at that arm of yours. How's it feelin' this morning?"

"It hurts, Pap! I got shot ya know? And I ain't a youngun no more. I'm older than Rusty, and I can sit guard on the porch, too. I want to help."

His off-handed but brutally honest answer brings a few laughs from around the table, including me. "Well, you're right. I guess you did get shot and you're dealing with it like a man, so I guess I ought not call you a youngun no more. But you lost some blood yesterday, and you still look a little pale. I think a day or two of rest are in order for you."

"Aw, man, I'm okay, and I want to help."

"No, your pap is right," states Becca. "You need to rest up a bit, youngun" she chides.

Grace glares at her. But before he can say anything, Becca coos in a loving gramma way, "You will always be a youngun to me, Grace." She bends over and kisses him on the forehead. "Now let's get a new bandage on that arm. Come on, Britt, we'll do it on the back porch were there's more light. Grab what we'll need from the bathroom."

Young Mark, and James, Janie's two youngest boys, six and eight years old, have listened to this conversation, stunned, and wide eyed. "Grace got shot!" exclaims James. "How did that happen? Are you going to be a soldier like my dad?" he asks Grace.

Janie chimes in. "There was a little accident when Pap was bringing them here yesterday, boys. Now how about we go outside and see if we can find duck eggs, okay? Come on, boys."

As she takes Sarah from Becca. I notice she has her shoulder holster on. No wallflower, that Janie. Smart girl.

Ken, Rusty, Blake and Larson are left in the kitchen with me. I get up to help finish cleaning up. I offer the last of

170

the scrambled eggs to the other two boys, and they hastily finish them off.

"You know those were farm eggs, not store eggs, don't you?"

Blake stops with his last forkful poised in front of his mouth, and looks at me quizzically, a little squint eyed, then exaggeratedly gobbles them down. "It's okay, Pap. I guess we may not get store eggs for a while."

I nod approvingly. "Blake, grab your 22, and go sit guard with Kim. Have Linc come up here so we can figure out what we need to get done today, and take this plate of food up for her, okay?"

"Sure, Pap," he says as he wipes his mouth. He grabs the plate and his 22 as he heads out the door.

"Ken, did you get a chance to come up with a guard duty roster?"

"Yeah, Mark, I got it right here." I look it over. It will work, with a few tweaks so that some chores can get done.

"I'll post this in my office. That's where the security system is and that will end up being our command post. Hey, there's Linc." I pull a plate of bacon and eggs from the oven. "Eat up, my new friend, we got lots to do."

The four of them are sitting at the large table as I pace in front of them and begin talking.

"Linc, this is all going to be new to you, but Ken and the boys know a lot about what's up, what we got here. As you all have seen, it's bad out there, the grid is down, chaos is going to happen, has already started to happen. We are not going to let chaos happen here. We are going to be a safe haven, a place where chaos is turned back. A place where normalcy will get a kickstart. But we can't help anyone if we can't help ourselves.

"Okay, first thing is to protect this safe haven. The security system is shot, but the electric is up and running, so is the water. The Faraday cage worked, as far as I know, or we wouldn't have electric. So everything in the Faraday cage should be good, too."

"Faraday cage?" Linc asks. "Metal enclosed box, grounded ten feet down? You got one of those? Really? I thought that was just theoretical stuff in books, and for the tinfoil hat conspiracy guys."

I open a drawer, and pull out a roll of tin foil, as I start to answer. "We don't really have a metal box, it's more of a metal shed." I rip off two sheets of foil from the roll. "We have back-up systems for most everything we may need." I begin to fold the sheet of foil. "There's a couple of old laptops in there, replacement cameras, a replacement controller for the cameras, some old monitors, an old dvd player or two. Even our old smart phones. If I could have afforded it, I would have put everything in there I needed to get my Dodge 2500 running, too." I place my pirate-style tinfoil hat on my head, and hand the other one to Linc. He looks at me a bit amused, and places the tinfoil pirate hat on his head. He smiles as he looks around at all of us smiling at him, nodding knowingly.

"You have got to be kidding me!" Linc says, still grinning. "We stumbled onto a group of tinfoil hat-wearing, Bible thumping, heavily armed, farmers who want to save the world? I'll be damned!"

"No, you have been blessed, Linc," my wife says as she enters the room. "And, Mark, you better unfold and wipe down that tin foil hat. I told you not to be doing that, that's a precious commodity you're playing with now, and you truly look like a fool." She blows me a kiss as she heads towards the bathroom.

"She took the words right out of my mouth, Linc. God put you here for a reason. I am sure you will be a blessing to us. But right now, we got to get the security system back up and running. Ken, you know where the cameras are, right?"

"There's one on the front porch of the farmhouse looking down the lane, there's one looking at the chicken coop, and one on the barn looking at the meadow where the cows graze. The last one is down the little draw looking at the old logging road, right? That one will be a little hard to find."

"Yep, but the one in the farmhouse is in the attic, and there are eight cameras in the cage, plus a controller, and about two thousand feet of co-ax wire with power cord, so we can set up a few more cameras. I want you to make sure we get those four cameras replaced, along with the controller and monitor. I am pretty sure that you can then run a line from here to the farmhouse, and get a laptop or monitor up there as a slave that will display everything that we see down here. That way we won't need someone here, and up there all the time."

"Aren't you going to be here to help?"

"No, I'm not. I'm going to Central City. I need to talk with Reverend Wysinger, and see what's going on. I'll take Larson with me."

"The girls are also going to need a lot of help organizing everyone, and getting things unpacked and stored. You boys, er, excuse me. You young men, help them out with anything they need."

Becca emerges from the hallway to the bathroom, "Remember, Grammy is the boss of Mark, which makes me the boss of you. Yes, I just said that, and I mean it," she says, heading back to the porch, with more antibiotic cream and tape.

"There's also eight wireless mic radios and a Ham radio in the cage. I got them cheap, off the internet. They're still in boxes. See if you can get them up and working. The Ham radio may need some kind of antenna. We will need to scrounge around and find what we need to build it. There's batteries and battery rechargers in the cage, too. Basically, check through all that stuff, and see what's working.

"Any questions guys?" I ask after finishing this ramble of things that need to be done.

"I guess I don't get to keep my tinfoil hat, huh? I think Kim would get a kick out of this!" Linc says, pointing at his new headgear. "I think it will help me let her know what kind of tinfoil hat-wearing freaks we have settled in with. I mean have been blessed by." We all laugh together at his good humor.

"Go show your wife your poor taste in hats, and let her know what we're doing today." Linc heads out, with a goofy grin that only a fifty-something year old guy wearing a tinfoil hat can get away with.

I glance over at Ken, as he watches this bit of silliness take place. I see a bit of a smile briefly cross his face. I silently thank God. We need Ken, we can't have him in a dark place.

Ken stands as I walk over to him. "I'm trusting my world to you, son," I say as I extend my hand. He grasps my hand and I pull him into a brief bro hug. "You got this?" I ask as we break our short embrace. "I'll make sure Becca knows what's going on, too. She knows this farm inside and out. She'll make sure all the chores get done, especially with a few grandsons to help her. I need you to work on that camera system, and the other electronics, okay?"

"I'm good, Mark," Ken responds. "I seen you working with the folks, they need a leader like you, you get to town, and help them out. We won't survive out here if the rest of the town goes to crap. Go make sure they got a handle on things, we'll be okay here."

I head out to the porch, where Britt and Becca are finishing up dressing Grace's arm, "So what's your assessment?" I ask.

"Well, there is no redness or excessive swelling that we can see, at least as far as we know, we've never dealt with a gun shot wound! But it's not infected, if that's what you're asking. We gave him the last antibiotic pill, so that's a bit of a worry." She stands, and looks directly at me. "Or are you asking about my assessment that you are going to town, leaving your family at a time like this? Shit just hit the fan and you're leaving your family! To go see if you can save the world! My assessment of that is not good. But I know that is what you are going to do. So go, we'll be okay." She turns away, crying. I turn her to me, and hug her tightly. At first she does not hug me back. But then she clings tightly. "Go! Do what you need to do, Mark, I know you have to. I love you." She turns back to finishing the bandage, lightly sobbing. I turn and head to get ready to go to Central City.

Chapter 23   Central City, Day 3, September 13. 2018

Larson is riding shotgun in the old van. He has an AR15 in his hands and an old 1911 45 caliber in a shoulder holster. Spare clips for both are in an old fishing vest I suited him up with as a makeshift combat vest. He is on edge, and that is good. After what we both witnessed yesterday, we know these roads are dangerous. I am glad to see him alert and concerned.

We pass Thad's farm and see his cows in the pasture. We see him out in a far field mowing hay. He must still have diesel. How long can the farmers keep producing? I think. How many farmers are going to start losing cows, and other livestock without transportation for feed. No refrigeration, no artificial insemination? What other parts of the food supply chain are going to break down with no modern technology? The cities are going to be hard hit because the food won't be able to be delivered. Generally speaking, three days of food supply is all that the stores have. And that is already being fought over.

Has the countryside become so reliant on modern technology that even farmers will have a hard time surviving? The big combines are all dead, electronics shot. Major swathes of cropland in the corn belt will go unharvested. The major food factories will be in trouble. The chicken farms, with hundreds of thousands of layers and meat birds, the pigs farms with automated feeding systems, all will be scrambling to keep just a portion of their flocks and herds. And how much of the country's crop is hybrid, unable to produce fertile seeds? Smaller farmers, like Thad, with older equipment, will become the nation's food source, those that survive. But does Thad grow heirloom crops? Will he have seed for next year? I am still pondering that question as we roll in sight of the Central City roadblock.

This roadblock is much different than what we passed the day before. They have moved several newer model cars into position to completely block the road from tree line to tree line. Two working farm trucks are set up behind the roadblock. A smaller car blocks an opening through the middle. I can see at least four armed guys manning the roadblock, and they scurry for cover as we approach. I stop a hundred yards short of them, glad to see their caution, but worried that someone might get an itchy finger. I should have thought to bring a white flag!

I step out of the van, unarmed, except for my pistol, hands held up. "Yo to the roadblock!" I holler. "Peaceful citizen wishing to pass through to see Reverend Wysinger!"

I see a guy from behind one of the farm trucks talking to another guy I didn't see before. After a few seconds, one of them hollers for me to come forward on foot, hands raised. I tell Larson not to worry, and I walk up to the roadblock, hands held high.

When I get about halfway there I hear someone holler to the man at the farm truck. "Hey, Jimmy, he's okay. That's the guy that bought all the water and food for the stragglers from me on the day this started." They talk a bit amongst themselves, and then the guy by the farm truck hollers for me to bring the van on up.

I hustle back to the van, and we drive up to the roadblock. The blocking car remains in place as I step out to greet the two men coming from the roadblock.

"Yep, Jimmy, this is the guy, he bought all that stuff, and gave it to the church for the relief effort." I recognize the young man from the store. I don't recognize Jimmy. Even in a small town, if you didn't grow up there, you're an outsider.

I stick out my hand, "Mark Mays, I got a farmstead outside of town. I was hoping to talk to Reverend Wysinger, and maybe whoever else is in charge here." The man takes my hand warily. "Jimmy Younger, and I'm in charge here. What's your business comin' here?"

"Well, Jim, like your friend over there said, I bought a bunch of supplies for the church to help some of the stragglers make it on to Johnstown. I also talked with Reverend Wysinger about setting up a relay system with the old farm trucks that are still running to move people on to Windber, or the Murtha Airport. I just wanted to see how that all worked out."

"Well, it worked out okay till those biker drug heads started killin' and rapin' anyone on the road. One of my boys got shot runnin' some of those stragglers to Windber. Good idea you had there, Saint Mark!" he says with anger. "And all that food and water, we supposed to give it away to strangers cause you say so? And now you want to say you're my friend!? Why don't you turn your ass around and get the hell out of my town, Saint Mark!"

I am taken aback by the hostility. This was not expected. I pause, as I silently ask God for guidance. Only open honesty and sincerity will diffuse this standoff. "You may not consider me your friend, Jimmy, but I am not your enemy. I didn't shoot your son. Your son was brave to help those strangers. And I bought those supplies for the stragglers to help move them through town. It's bad here right now, Jimmy. If the electricity doesn't come back on, how bad do you think it will be in a couple of weeks, if we have a few thousand extra people here?"

"We coulda turned those folks back at the other roadblocks," Jimmy replies. "Don't matter anyhow now. Ain't no one moving nowhere. Those druggie bikers got all the roads shut down. Been a bunch of people robbed and killed up on Route 30. "

"Well, those druggies shot his brother yesterday," I say pointing at Larson in the van. "Come look at these bullet holes," I say, showing him where we got shot up. "And his old man," I say, pointing at Larson again, "He shot five of them assholes on the other side of Hooversville. They tried to ambush us, but we ambushed them. I might not be your friend, Jimmy, but I ain't your enemy."

Jimmy fingers the holes in the side of the van, and ponders for a bit. He turns, and eyes me up again, silently, anger still in his eyes. "Mark Mays, you say. I heard you're a stand up man. You did work for my sister. I remember her saying you stood by your work, did a good job." He stares off into the distance for a bit. "You're right, Mark, you didn't shoot my son. He was trying to do good, and those meth heads shot him. He'll be okay, and it wasn't your fault. I'm just pissed as hell at what's going on. People are dying, people are gettin' kilt for no reason! Guess I'm taking out my anger on you. We need to band together, to keep out these bad folks. You go on into town, maybe you can help all these folks get things straightened out."

I shake Jimmy's hand again, this time with warmth. He waves the blocking car away from the roadblock and we move on through.

***

We have barely seen any human activity out on the county roads, but here in town, things are happening. People are moving cars off to the side of the road, An old tow truck is moving some of the cars, presumably for more roadblocks. Many people are visibly carrying side arms, and some are carrying long guns. There is an orderly line in front of the pharmacy, and the doctor's office; armed civilians watching over both establishments. There is a large crowd of people at the fire hall and their community barbeque pit is billowing smoke. I see another large group of people at the Baptist Church, as well as the two other churches.

I pull into the church parking lot, next to two older farm trucks. Each truck has an armed civilian standing next to it. "Let's see what's going on here, Larson. Sling that rifle like you know what you're doing, son. Stand tall, okay?" I say seriously.

He looks at me, gives a serious nod, and steps out of the van. We introduce ourselves to the other vehicle guards, and are soon on friendly terms. They indicate that things are pretty much okay, but that a few stragglers tried to take a vehicle yesterday, so everyone is being very watchful. I leave Larson with his new friends, to watch our van, and I head into the church. There are close to several hundred people waiting in food lines, or curled up in blankets around the church. It's mainly calm, but surreal and depressing. The despair is seen on the faces of those waiting for help, stranded, with no way home.

I'm met at the church door by a smiling woman I recognize, but I can't remember her name. "Come on in, Mark," she says. "What can we do for you?"

"I'd like to speak with Reverend Wysinger, if he's available."

"He and the deacons are just finishing up a meeting. I'll let him know you are here. By the way, what you did with all those supplies for the needy, I think you have a heart of gold." She quickly turns, and heads down a side hallway.

Another man is standing just outside the door, seemingly guarding the place, but he is unarmed. He stares silently over the church property, barely even taking notice of me, keeping his attention on what's going on outside. I wait silently.

I see several men coming from the hallway the woman went down. One is Jerry, my shotgun rider from yesterday. "Hey, Jerry! Nice to see you, friend!" We grasp each other in a big bear hug. "How are things here?" I ask.

He steps back and frowns, "Not good, not good. Those meth heads we ran into yesterday, that was just one group of many. They're terrorizing the countryside. A few of those relay trucks we set up got shot up, and they have Route 30 shut down from what we can figure. These refugees, those that made it here, they're stuck here for now. We can take care of them for a few days, but we need to look after our own, too. And there is probably a couple thousand still at Flight 93, with no food and limited water. Those meth heads, they're highway bandits on drugs, literally. We got to do something about them."

"I'm about to meet with the reverend. I know you got a good head on your shoulders, come back with me, help me get up to speed on the situation, maybe figure some things out." He nods and turns to head back with me to see the reverend.

The woman whose name I can't remember lets us know the reverend can see us, and smiles as we enter his office. Reverend Wysinger stands and shakes my hand warmly. "Good to see you, Mark, good to see you. And thank you so much for what you have done. We'll be able to take care of these folks for a few more days, thanks to you and a few donations from some of our farmers." He stands back. "It's bad, Mark, real bad. Jerry told me what you went through. Those bandits hit the outskirts of town, and ran up on one of our roadblocks, too. Thank God we moved the roadblocks out to the town limits, or they would have shot up the town, like they did in Hooversville. Still, they shot up a couple of our trucks runnin' folks to Windber. That was a good idea, but we had to shut it down. Now we're trying to figure out what we can do. Those yahoos have us hemmed in, and we have a bunch of people here that we won't be able to feed soon."

He sits down, exasperated. We all look at each other silently, the enormity of the situation setting in. Why are we still here? I ask myself. "Let's pray, Reverend, we need God's guidance. We need to pray." I reach my hands out, and the three of us clasp hands and bow our heads.

I begin, "Dear Lord, we are here for a reason, and you have a path you want us to follow, show us the path, allow us to use the talents you have blessed us with to glorify your kingdom, allow us to help those in need, and make wise decisions in dealing with those who would pursue a path of evil"… for ten minutes, the three of us pour out our hearts to the Lord. We pray that the power may be restored, that the people who wish evil upon us may turn their hearts, and give up their path of evil. We pray that we might find the resources to feed those in our care, the locals and the refugees. We ask for wisdom and guidance, forgiveness and grace. The reverend finishes,"We ask your mercy, Lord, in Christ's name we do pray, Amen."

We break hands, and sit back silently, calmly. No miracles have suddenly happened, the electricity didn't suddenly come back on. The drug addicts didn't all lay down their arms, and come to the church. A truckload of food didn't just roll into town.

"So what do we do now?" Jerry asks.

"Who's in charge, Jerry? I know some of the things you and I suggested on the roadblocks have happened. The churches are helping with the refugees and the fire department has food for the people. Who is organizing all that?"

"Chief Speigle and me kind of got the roadblocks organized. I set up the roadblocks, and he set up the manpower, just from local folk who wanted to help. There where plenty of men once word of what happened in Hooversville and the killin's on Route 30 got around. The mayor has been trying to help out, but he has been more of a nuisance than anything else."

"The mayor did get the fire department to start the free barbeque with the food from the grocery that's for locals and volunteers," says the reverend. "And the three churches banded together to set up the refugee stations. We are a bit frowned on by some of the locals, figuring we ought to save the food and water for them. Father Keith shot himself, so that has added some turmoil, but the congregation is still trying to help out."

"You had a guy with a Ham radio, any word from him?" I ask. The reverend shakes his head.

"So we got food and water for people for now, and we got security set up. But with these meth heads runnin' the roads, everything is bottled up. We can't sit here waiting to starve to death because some road warriors from Mad Max want to kill and rape. We have to put a stop to that. There's plenty of farms with food, so we can take care of ourselves, but we need freedom to move and trade."

We all sit quietly again for a spell. "Anyone talk to Johnny at the VFW?" Jerry asks. We both look at him quizzically. "There are a bunch of young vets from around here," he responds. "They won't take lightly to the country they fought for being taken over by a bunch of druggies. We need to talk with him."

"Johnny who?" I ask.

"John Fisher, Johnny, he's a retired First Seargeant, Army Ranger. Everyone calls him Top. He is a solid guy, everyone respects him, the vets at the VFW, that is."

We make plans. The reverend will continue to unite the churches in helping the refugees, and coordinate with the mayor to keep tensions down. Jerry will talk with the VFW about recruiting some concerned vets to deal with the road bandits. I'm going to try and find out more about what's going on in the countryside, and see if we can get more food to the town for the locals, and the refugees. We agree to meet at the township building the next day, at noon. Reverend Wysinger is a little leery of having his church used as a base of operations.

As we break up our little meeting, the lights come on in the church. We all look around, Huh, is it over? The nice lady opens the door excitedly. "Sorry to interrupt, but one of our parishioners just finished setting up a generator for us, we should be able to run everything in the church, including the kitchen and refrigerators! Thank God for small miracles!" We all look at each other and smile in disbelief.

***

I talk with Larson a bit outside the church to find out what news he heard while we were inside. He tells me the farm trucks were able to run about a hundred people to Windber before they got ambushed, which happened yesterday afternoon. He points out a guy who was driving one of the trucks. He also points out a group of people sitting on a large blanket under a tree, refugees. He tells me their story. Their group was ambushed on the road. They ran into the woods to escape. They saw four men shot, two were alive but the bandits executed them. Three woman and two children were carried off in a van. The women were violated right there on the road, before they loaded them up. He has the look in his eye that his father did, after we got ambushed. He should be looking forward to his senior year in high school, thinking about college and a career. He's a talented musician and loves the theater. Now he is dealing with the chaos that comes when there is no law, no morality.

I look him straight in the eye. "We'll get through this, Larson. God has not left us, but this is what happens when you have no God. The people that ambushed those folks, they are godless. But God will prevail, the good in all of us will prevail."

He looks at me sternly, "Bad shit is happening, Pap, bad shit. We got to stop them."

I walk over to talk with the driver who was in the refugee caravan that got ambushed. Then I spend some time talking with the group of refugees. Both tales are similar in that it was chaos. No organization on either side. In the truck ambush, two trucks came up on the caravan form the opposite direction, and just started shooting. Our guys were on their way back to Central City so the lead truck just gunned it, and the other three followed suit. The bandits didn't have enough time to turn around, and inflict any real damage. But that was when Jimmy's son got hit, he was driving the second truck in line. The refugees report a similar tale. Two trucks pulled up and just started shooting, total chaos. They ran into the woods, and those left on the road were killed or taken. The bandits hollered at them from the road, but never pursued them into the woods. Then they mounted up, and just took off, shootin' and hollerin' as they went. I question as to whether the attackers were drinkin' or looked hyped up. The answer is a definite yes. I also get descriptions of the trucks they were driving. Each time the bandits had two trucks, but they were not the same trucks in each attack.

I hook back up with Larson, and we head out to the roadblock where they had a run-in with the bandits. The roadblock is on Route 160, just outside of town, and a few miles north of Route 30, the road that Flight 93 Memorial is on. The roadblock is well placed, at a wooded chokepoint; four cars block the road from wood line to wood line. The road is very straight here, and rises slightly away from town. There is a working farm truck placed heading into town. I see several people in a heated discussion. They all stop and turn to us as we drive up. I stop about twenty yards short of their position, arriving from the protected side. There is no hostility towards us, but they are alert and curious.

I step out, leaving my long gun in the van. "Yo friends, Jerry sent me up here to check on you all, and ask about your run-in with the druggies." The Jerry reference calms things a bit, a few smiles appear. I recognize one of the four men from a local lumber store. "Barry! What's up, friend! Great to see you." I give him a big bro hug, then step back, and assess the crew. Three have deer rifles, one a pump shotgun. Two have side arms. I see two more on lookout with scoped deer rifles. They have a water jug set up in the back of a farm truck. I see some debris from snacks they had been eating, probably from the gas station a few hundred yards back.

Barry introduces me to his three compadres. I have Larson fetch some apples from our van for everyone. The mood lightens. We begin to exchange stories and news. I offer up a brief version of the Moxham fire, and our ambush outside of Hooversville. They look at Larson, impressed, even though it was his dad who took the shots. He swells a bit with pride, but still has a bit of grimness about him that I have never seen before.

They start talking about the run-in they had yesterday. Two of the guys were here when it all went down. They had set up the roadblock about noon. Just two cars across the pavement. People had been coming in from the Flight 93 Memorial, and they had talked of some bad things happening on Route 30, so chief Speigle had them set up the roadblocks.

About noon, they heard shooting, kind of far away. They would hear more shooting now and again, sometimes closer, sometime farther away. Then there was a bit of a rush of refugees, all of them talking about a couple of trucks shootin' up people on the road, and lootin' the stores, taking hostages. Then the refugees stopped, at about six o'clock. No more people coming down the road. By this time they had six guys up on the roadblock, and had sent a couple into the woods on both sides of the road. Shortly later, two trucks came over the rise, traveling fast. They slowed, and stopped about five hundred yards away when they saw the roadblock. Then they just sped up straight at the roadblock. They started shootin' the whole place up, but wild like. One of the guys at the roadblock had served in Afghanistan, and kept them all cool. He had them all start firing when the druggies were about one hundred yards out. When the druggies realized they were getting shot at, they did quick one-eighties and turned tail. Two fell dead out of one of the trucks when they turned, and one truck almost crashed heading back out, like the driver had been shot. The description of the trucks matched that of what the refugees had described on Route 30.

I congratulated them on turning back this impromptu assault, told them that it would keep the druggies back, looking for softer targets. I also warned them that they may get scouted, and to make sure they keep people posted about two hundred yards ahead of the roadblock in the woods.

As we are standing there talking, one of the guards hollers that two people can be seen coming down the road. We all stop talking, and turn to see what's up. A guy hollers at us to take secure positions. We do so.

A tall scraggly guy with a smaller thin woman can be seen hobbling towards us. Their clothes are dirty and torn. They look sickly. The man has a walking stick, and is holding the woman tightly around the waist. About two hundred yards away, the man rips off what is left of his t-shirt, and ties it to his walking stick, he waves it high in the air, and starts to holler. "Don't shoot! Don't shoot! My girl's pregnant, and she needs help! Don't shoot!" We see no firearms. The lead man waves them forward.

A few minutes later, the couple hobbles through the gap, and into safety; and interrogation. These two do not look like refugees. Tattoos, piercings, sunken eyes, goth type dress, these two are druggies.

"Where'd you all come from?" asks Barry.

"Back yonder," the guy responds. "Back up the road." His eyes can't focus, and he doesn't make eye contact with anyone. "My girl is pregnant, and she is real sick, we need help," he pleads.

"Barry, let's get them to town, she's in bad shape, maybe a miscarriage. I want to talk with them, they won't bring no harm. I'll see to that."

Chapter 24 More Central City, Day 3, September 13, 2018

We get our two druggie refugees to Central City. We take them to the townhall, and I send Larson out to find Jerry, or Chief Speigle. A local woman, who is a nurse, begins to check them over. She checks on the woman first. She slowly strips away her ragged clothing, and starts asking her questions. The young girl has clearly been abused, physically, and sexually; blood and bruises show that she has been roughed up.

They begin to tell their story to us, as the nurse continues her check up. They are from Greensburg, were at a friend's cabin for the weekend. They were just having fun, doing some drugs. With no job to go back to, they decided to stay an extra few days. The freedom of the girl's morals helped pay the way for them to stay. Then the lights went out.

They stayed at that camp for about a day, then someone came around, said that they needed to get all their stuff, and move to this big compound. This guy said the power was down forever, and that this new group was going to rule the area, that they were already out getting food and drugs for everyone. The young man would be a soldier, and the woman could be his wife, they would be okay, especially if the wife continued to be rather friendly.

Jerry, Chief Speigle, and a man I recognize, but don't know, step into the room. Introductions are made, and I find out the new man is John Fisher, First Sergeant, retired army ranger, First Calvary division. I give them all a brief recap about the two druggies before us. The young man continues with his story.

Not knowing what to do, they went to this new compound. It's a big farm, with horses, cows and several buildings. There were already about twenty people there, many with bikes, and some old farm trucks too. He tells us that the farm trucks go out in pairs on supply runs. Each time they come back, they bring food, liquor drugs, women, and children.

He says that he and his girl stayed liquored up and hyped on meth, just fell into the flow of things. But it was bad, he says. The women and children being brought back were forced to do things, then they saw how pretty his girl was, and they forced her to do things, too. He was forced to go out on a supply trip and was told to just kill the men, bring back the women and children, and anything they had worth keeping.

That night, yesterday, he heard about some of the supply people getting shot up, and that they all had to get ready to take the town in retaliation. The head man, who he described as small and squirrelly, but very mean, said they couldn't have some townsfolk holding out, that they needed to raid the town so they could raid the drug stores and bars; that they needed to teach the people a lesson.

Later, the tall lean druggie continues, his girl came back to their tent, and sha had been really roughed up. She said she would have treated them right, but that they wanted to treat her bad. That's when she told him she thought she may be pregnant, that she may have had a miscarriage. They both decided they needed to leave.

The next morning, when they had a chance, they grabbed an ATV, and traveled the back paths until they got to a main road. But the ATV ran out of gas, so they started walking, and ended up at the roadblock.

The nurse steps in, grimfaced. "She has had a miscarriage. She's lost a lot of blood, and there is redness and swelling, infection. She is also going through withdrawals."

I look at the man before us. He has turned even paler, and is showing signs of withdrawal, too. "Can we get some antibiotics from the pharmacy? There's a methadone clinic at the edge of town, can we get a few hits from them?"

"Maybe, but who's going to pay for this?" the nurse responds.

"They came to us for help, we have to help them, if we can." I dig into my wallet, cash is getting short after the big splurge at the dollar store. "Will two hundred bucks cover what we need?"

The First Sergeant pulls out another hundred dollars, and hands it to the nurse. "Tell Maggie at the clinic to make sure to take care of them, this is important." The nurse looks at the cash, then at us, she nods, and heads back out the door.

The First Sergeant looks at the strung-out man. "Young man, we will do what we can to save your girl and you, but you need to tell us everything you saw at that compound you were at. We have already made a commitment to help you and your girl, now it's your turn to help us."

"You don't understand, sir, I'll help all I can. Those people are evil! And now I've lost a son! Help me please, help my girl! I'll tell you everything."

I look at Jerry, the First Sergeant, and Chief Speigle. "You all got this. I got a farm to run, and a family to look after. You all know where I am, send word if you need me." They nod in unison. I feel confident that they will take good care of our two informants. I head back outside.

Larson and I swing past the church, and I briefly talk with the reverend, telling him of all we have learned. He lets me know that if we can't open up the roads, and move the refugees on, food will get short.

We climb back in the van, I let Larson know we are taking a route out towards Route 30, and then follow some back roads east, to the farmstead. I want to see what's going on up towards Route 30, where the trouble seems to be happening. I tell him to keep alert, that we will hit the gas, and run if we see any trouble. He nods, his AR15 gripped firmly.

***

We head out past the roadblock that had been hit the day before, our tensions rising as we are heading into no-man's land. We crest the hill well past the roadblock, and see the road almost completely blocked! But this isn't a roadblock, this is a cattle drive!

We pull off to the side of the road as about thirty milk cows, heavy in the udder, start to pass by. There are two young men, teenagers, moving the cattle, along with an older girl, maybe twenty, in a wagon pulled by a horse. "What's up, men?" I holler from the van as they pass by.

One of the young men stops to talk with me. "We can't milk and feed all the cows. Pop said for us to move these cows into town. Sell 'em if we can. They're gonna go dry if we keep them on the farm. We can't milk 'em all, and we won't have enough feed for them through the winter. We also got milk and butter in the wagon. Ain't pasteurized, but it's better that way, I say."

"You take these cows to Reverend Wysinger at the Baptist Church. He may not be able to pay you for them, but have him give you a voucher for thirty cows that you gave to the community. Your generosity will be noted. He'll take care of you, sooner or later. I see you're armed, stay alert, there's been bad trouble on some of these roads. You see trouble coming, you run, don't wait to see if they're friendly folks, okay?" They nod as they continue on to town.

A mile further up the road we turn left, and start taking country roads back to the farmstead. We stop and talk with a few folks we see. We let them know about the meth-heads, and warn them to be wary. Almost all of them are carrying side arms at this point. The third day, and people are starting to realize that things are different.

Larson and I make our round about way back to the farmstead, and pull down the country lane about midafternoon.

Chapter 25   Moxham to Davidsville, Day 3 Herc's Story, September 13, /2018

Herc has an old lawn tractor with a trailer, and a spare five-gallon can of gas. They will head up the hill towards Richland, and the better neighborhoods, where there are less drug dealers and hoodlums. He is a skilled guy, he can get work up there, until they get settled in, he thinks.

"Leesa. you're right, we gotta go. And we won't be back. Pack everything you can that will fit in the garden trailer. I'm packing my guns and tools, too, so that won't leave much room. We're leavin' as soon as we can."

They pack up in the dark of night. Some clothes, some food, some of Herc's tools that he saved from his house, and the rest of the available room for Herc's guns and ammo. They also pack a rucksack that Herc will wear as he walks alongside the garden tractor that Leesa will drive, with John Jr. in the trailer.

They head out at first light. They tell no one they are going. They just head off to higher ground, hopefully safer ground. They leave behind smoldering fires, occasional gunshots, and the putrid smell of death and destruction. Wayward travelers in a new world.

***

It is early in the third morning after the power went out. Herc walks with Leesa driving the lawn tractor, the trailer, and John Jr. in tow, with all they own. Herc carries his 30/30 on a swivel sling with his twelve gauge pump action shotgun strapped to his back, and his Colt 1911 45mm tucked in the back of his belt. Leesa has a .38 in a shoulder holster and a scoped 270 sitting on her lap. He fears nothing, and everything, at the same time. They make good time heading up the hill, away from Moxham.

They pass the remains of the concrete truck, fuel truck collision, and see the scars left by the fire still burning further up the hill. Many other people are heading up the hill, too. Some totally unprepared, just walking away from the mayhem below. Others are leaving town like Herc and Leesa, full back packs, bicycles with trailers, wheelbarrows full of belongings. There is a definite migration away from the valley, and the chaos that is consuming it.

By the time they make it to Scalp Avenue, the main drag through Richland, and the main shopping districts, the sun is fully up, and more people are out and about. No one pays them much attention. A plan is formulating between Leesa and Herc. Leesa is a paralegal, and has some connections with a few well-off people in Richland. They hope those connections will help out. Realizing legal services won't be in high demand, she will offer services as a nanny or housemaid, and Herc will try to earn some money as a handy man. Hopefully they will find a place to stay and they get settled in.

Just before noon, they are heading towards the intersection of Route 219 and Scalp Avenue. They are squarely in the middle of the main shopping area for all of Johnstown. Looting of stores is going on around them as they slowly roll down the road. A few stores are defended by armed men, and the looters, or scavengers, stay away from them. The people here look more desperate, not as angry. They are looking for food, not revenge or control, as they where in Moxham. Most people pay no attention to Herc and his family. The few that turn his way, quickly look elsewhere when they see he is well armed, and carries a determined look.

At the 219 overpass, he sees a roadblock has been set up. He has Leesa stop with their tractor, about 100 yards short of the roadblock. He gives Leesa the 30/30, and approaches the roadblock. His pistol is in his belt, his shot gun is in his raised hand, finger held well away from the trigger, the other hand held high, too.

Herc is not much of a talker, so he keeps heading toward the roadblock expecting a warm reception. About fifty yards away he is told to stop by a large man in a cop uniform. "What business you got comin' up here?" The large cop hollers.

"Me and my wife and kid got nowhere to go. My house burned down in Moxham, and my family got killed down there. I can work construction, and my wife, she's a paralegal and knows some people up here. She can clean houses, and stuff like that. We're willing to work if someone will put us up."

"You ain't the only ones that's offered that," replies the large cop. "This is a gun-free zone. We can try to help you, but you got to give up your arms. Both you and the woman have to disarm, then maybe we can take you in."

Herc stands there in the middle of the road, looking at the roadblock, hands still held high. "I can fight, officer. I know my weapons, I'll help you on your guard post." There is some discussion among a few people at the roadblock.

"Don't want to be turning down help., but we don't know you. If you want through, you got to disarm. We don't want all that lootin' on this side of the highway. We all decided this is our stand. Those are the rules. You can come in, but you got to disarm. Maybe after we get to know you, you can join our guard."

Herc looks around. He has always been a self-reliant man who has never made quick decisions. His weapons have set him apart from others. His weapons saved what is left of his family. He don't see givin' up his weapons as a good idea. He watches as a desperate couple walks thru the roadblock. The man hands over a 12 gauge single shot, and a small caliber pistol. They are quickly welcomed, and led off, past his field of view.

No, he decides. He will not be reliant on these people. He has food for a while, and he can defend himself and his family.

"Ain't givin up my weapons," he hollers at the officer. "They're the only reason me and my family are still alive. We'll head south on the highway."

The cop eyes him up, eyes up Leesa, and John Jr. on their overloaded tractor. He tells the men at the roadblock to stand down as he walks out to talk with Herc.

As the cop approaches, he extends a hand, "Jeff Hays. If you're heading south, I want to tell you what I know."

"Herc," Herc grasps his hand as Leesa comes up with the lawn tractor. "That's my girl, Leesa and boy, John Jr."

The cop looks around a bit nervously. He looks at Herc, a bit questioningly.

"Whatever you got to say to me, they can hear it too, we're all headin' the same way."

"We took in a few hundred people, they come up from the Flight 93 Memorial. They all showed up the first night, after it all went dark. Since then, we got in only a couple dozen people. All of them are talking about some crazed dudes. Bad stuff, if you know what I mean," he says, looking at Leesa, and John Jr. with a rueful eye. "Most of the bad shit has happened on Route 30, and the back roads. The army, just a few hours ago, started running patrols up and down 219 to Somerset and back. But they only have a few vehicles running. I asked them about heading back to the Flight 93 Memorial. They say that's going to be their next move, but it may be a few days. If you get off Route 219, you're in no man's land."

"We're heading south. You ain't got no reason to stop us, do you?" Herc responds frankly, mind made up.

"No sir, just wanted you to be aware."

Herc nods. "I can take care of me and mine, always have, always will." He motions to Leesa, and they head off together down Route 219, south. All they own is in a lawn tractor and trailer, with little John glancing around at the far off views of the western Pennsylvania mountains. Smoke plumes can be seen in several directions. Herc shakes his head in disgust as to what has happened to the world. Then he focuses on what is next, Route 219 South.

***

There is very little traffic on 219, foot traffic that is. Nor are there any farm trucks or old bikes. Basically nothing. Herc sees a few walkers in each direction, maybe ten in total over the two mile stretch he can see. That's not good, he thinks. Why haven't more people started heading towards the highway?

They walk for several hours, covering the eight miles to the Davidsville exit. Twice they are passed by a couple of old Hummers that slow down and check them over as they roll by. Dusk will be coming on before they get to the next exit. His gas can is half empty now. Maybe they can find some good people in Davidsville. They walk down the exit that takes them to Route 403.

At the bottom of the hill, blocking the way to State Route 403, is another roadblock. Herc is not surprised, it is where a roadblock should be. He stops several hundred yards away. He pulls up his field binoculars, and eyes up the scene. The roadway, with berms and grass, is almost fifty yards wide. The roadblock is very haphazard, but efficient. An old boat on a trailer, several cars, an RV. Much less organized than the

Richland roadblock, but much more effective, mainly because of the manpower he sees.

At least five folk move to a ready position as he comes into their view. He figures there has to be at least five more already in position, as he scouts the landscape. Another dozen are milling around, getting food from a truck, glancing his way, and pointing this way and that. Not a black skin to be seen. Herc is not a racist, but he is a realist. Twenty-five armed white guys looking at one well-armed black man with his inter-racial family. This needs to be handled delicately.

He grabs his white bandana off his head, and ties it to his 30/30. He waves it high over his head. "Can me and my family get safe rest here?" he hollers.

He sees a few long guns rest easy as a few others talk amongst themselves. After a few moments, one hollers for them to come closer. Herc brings his small caravan up to about one hundred yards from the roadblock. He is in no-mans land. If they open up on him, he and his family are done. But he doesn't have much choice. He stops again, waving his white flag atop his 30/30. "Can we have a safe place for the evening? We have our own food, we just want a safe place to stay," Herc hollers.

Two men come out from the roadblock, one younger, one older. Another comes down from a hidden position on the hillside. The one that comes down from the hidden position is as black-skinned as Herc. He steps up before the two from the roadblock arrive.

"Lay your weapons down, and raise your hands." The other black man states firmly, he has a 30.06 pointed squarely at Herc's chest. Herc lays down his weapons, and steps aside. He doesn't like this at all. He is almost completely defenseless.

The two from the roadblock jog up, and check over the scene. "Shit, Frank. You got this handled," the younger one says to the black man.

Frank looks at him and nods, "Doin' my job." The 30.06 still held steady at Herc's chest.

"You ain't part of them raider druggie folk, huh?" the older man asks Herc.

"I ain't no druggie, sir, I'm just trying to move my family out of the bad spots. Our house got burned down in Moxham, and my momma and brother got killed. I killed those bastards, but we heard they was comin back after us, so we left. We won't be no trouble, we're just lookin' for a safe place to sleep."

The man looks him over, looks into Herc's clear determined eyes, sees his hard strong muscles, and knows he is looking at a good man, not a druggie. He looks to Frankie, who nods and lowers his gun. Frankie steps forward and gives Herc a bro hug. He whispers in his ear "Welcome, friend. You'll be safe here."

***

Herc quickly gathers his firearms, and motions his family forward. They pass thru the roadblock, and are greeted warmly by several women who seem to be in charge of refugees. They are directed down the hill, to the small village of Benson. The large Methodist church there has a kitchen set up for those in need. Herc and his family get a warm meal. They sit down next to a woman they learn is trying to get home to Central City. A man passing by hears of her predicament. He says that they are looking to run a convoy through to Hooversville in the morning. There have been ambushes on the road to Hooversville, so they are going to send a group through armed and ready. A few others need to go that way, and they want to keep that road open despite the troubles that have been going on. He has heard of ambushes and shootouts on that road the day before.

Herc volunteers to ride as an armed guard on the convoy if he can take his family with him. His boss has a farmstead outside Central City. He knows he and his family will be welcome there, until he can figure out what to do. He has worked for Mark Mays since Mark first started his business. He knows Mark will help him and his family.

His offer to help guard a run to Hooversville is taken into consideration. Herc and his family are offered sleeping quarters on cots in the church, along with several dozen other refugees.

Chapter 26   Home Again, September 13, 2018

I am relieved of a great burden as we drive down the old lane to the farmstead. There is no smoke rising or any other signs that renegades have been about. As we come in sight of the old farmhouse porch, I see Rusty and Jodie standing alertly, firearms in hand. Janie is talking into a wireless mic. Great! Ken found some of the other goodies in the Faraday cage and has them up and working.

Janie waves happily, as little Sarah appears from behind the porch pillar, and shyly waves, too. We drive on back to the old barn and park. Becca comes running from the house, and bear hugs me, almost knocking me over. She kisses me deeply.

"Whoa! Wow, I'll take short trips away more often if I get a reception like that every time I come home!" I say, as she steps back to look me over. "Nothing happened, babe, no bullet wounds, we're both okay."

"You! If I didn't love you so much, I could slap you!" She hugs me again, then steps back. "You got stuff you never told me about. These wireless mics, with the control station, the extra cameras, and cable. No wonder you kept saying 'money was tight.'" She looks at, me a bit pissed, but then she smiles. She looks up with arms spread wide. "Thank you, God, for bringing this man into my life." She looks back at me warmly, and we embrace. "Now, tell me what's going on in town, and I'll tell you what we got done around here." She takes my hand, and we head back to the front porch of the new house. I send Larson off to have Ken, Britt and Jodie meet us there.

I tell them all briefly about our morning. There is some shock as to how things have turned chaotic in the countryside with the renegades running wild. I point out how rapidly things can deteriorate, when bad people know there will be no consequences for their actions. If people have no moral compass to guide them, and no threat of retaliation for their actions, then their worst characteristics can come forth.

Becca points out that God did answer our prayers. The lights did come back on; at the church. Two of the bad guys turned themselves in, willing to provide information. And a truckload of food was being delivered to town in the form of a herd of cattle. "God has not left us, he is watching over those who know him." As usual, my wife is right, prayers are being answered.

Her words make my mind wander a bit. We so often overlook how God answers prayers. Our prayers may not be answered in the way we expect, nor in the time we would like. But God always hears our prayers, and he always answers them. But we look at life through blinders, at our day-to-day problems, too focused on the small things to see how He is working in our lives, and in the world; everyday He is working miracles, answering our prayers. So how does that square with the power shutting down. Is that God working miracles? How so? Millions of people are going to die.

My faith is not shaken at these thoughts. He has provided a path for us, and we will follow that path. We will help all that we can as we walk in our faith. But what of those with no faith? Where will their path lead? And what about those with faith, trapped in a hopeless situation, in the big cities? I pray for them, I cannot help them. I need to concentrate on those I can help.

My growling stomach turns my thoughts away from deep matters, to the here and now. "Let's get some lunch, and you all can tell me what you got done while I was gone."

Becca and Janie head into the house to put some lunch together. I fire up a precious smoke, and offer one to Ken. Surprisingly, he takes me up on the offer.

"So you got the wireless mic system set up, I see. They'll work for up to about a half-mile. What about the cameras, and the control station?" I ask.

"Well, first I set up the recharging system, and main control station for the wireless mics. That's in your office, or 'command center,' here in the new house. I'd like to figure out how to get a remote station for that up in the old farmhouse. All the electronics you got stored in there! Crap, Mark, did you just put every old computer, laptop and monitor in that cage? I may be able to piece it together." I nod at his question, once the Faraday cage was set up, all old electronics got stacked in there.

Ken continues. "We got the front porch camera replaced, and two others. We didn't get to the one on the lower field. I just got started on replacing the controller system, and the remote display in the farmhouse. From what I am finding, we should be able to do it all. Running the cable for more cameras will be the hardest part."

"Can we get two cameras out on the county road, one looking in each direction? That could give us a big edge, if the renegades come scouting."

"Let me get the main controller up and running first. If that boots up, we can have eight cameras rolling, so two out on the county road shouldn't be a problem if we have the cable to do it." Ken responds.

I turn and look to Britt. "How's Grace doing?"

She's looking at the floor. "He's a bit anxious. He wants to be helping." She looks up. "Is this what we have to look forward to? Setting up a fortress, hunkering down, trying to

204

live off the land, collecting duck eggs, picking elderberries? I'm not ready for this!" She pauses a moment, tears forming in her eyes. Her words come fast and passionately. "My family is supposed to share a house with another family, and maybe more? My boy is riding shotgun as you go joy riding through the countryside? This ain't right!" Almost yelling now she continues, "My other boy got a gunshot wound, and we can't take him to the hospital? I watched as my husband had to gun down five men." She starts to weep heavily. We are all silent as she gets up, and hurries into the house. We all understand, we will all deal with this situation differently. Ken gets up and follows her, wiping a tear from his eye. He returns a few minutes later, his face is pale, and the stress he is feeling is seen in his stiff movements.

We sit quietly for a bit, shaken by Britt's honest outburst. Shortly, Janie comes out on the porch with lunch, thick slabs of tomato with goat cheese and basil leaves, a bit of olive oil drizzled over it all, with fresh pepper and salt. "We got lunch!" I look at the plate as a gourmet meal, and dig in. Ken says a short grace, and tentatively begins to nibble at the food before him. Janie steps back, a bit aghast. "You men think that rabbit food is a good lunch?"

I look up at her, "Janie, the days of pizza, and chicken nuggets are over. You got to eat what is available to eat, and this is mighty fine eatin'! Don't knock it till you try it. And your boys are going to look up to you, as to what to do. If you won't eat it, neither will your boys. Just saying, ya know." I dig into my thick slabs of tomato and basil, not looking back.

From the corner of my eye I see her slice the tomato, and tentatively take a bite. I see her cut a bigger piece of tomato and swipe it through the olive oil and pepper, stabbing a piece of basil. Shortly she is halfway through the big plate. I turn and smile at her. "I been telling you for years, this is great food! Tonight we get some zucchini with fresh peppers and onions!"

She scowls at me, "I didn't say I like it, I'm just hungry." With that statement she gobbles down the last of the food on her plate.

Becca joins us on the porch, clearly stressed. "Britt is not dealing with this well. She won't talk to me, and just sits, staring straight ahead, unresponsive."

"She'll be okay," states Ken. "I believe you Mays women call it processing. She'll work through it. The main thing is to make sure Grace heals up okay. That's what has her most worried. He should be on antibiotics. The EMT in Hooversville only gave him a few doses, those are gone.

"We got antibiotics!" exclaims Becca. "There's ampicilin, not more than six months old, in the medicine cabinet. Remember, Mark? From when you had your gums worked on?" She heads back into the house, on a mission to help her daughter feel better, and her grandson get better.

***

"Let's put a better perspective on this situation. Ken, Janie, you need to take a walk with me around the property. You know we have been setting the farm up as a safe place for something like this. But as the head of your families here, you need to know what we actually have, what we can do, and what needs to be done." They look at me, and nod, curiosity apparent on their faces. "Janie, go tell Becca I'm taking you on an inventory walk, she'll know what you mean. Let her know to look after the two boys. You can bring Sarah with us. Linc and Kim are working on setting up the main controller for the cameras?" I ask Ken, turning to him.

"Yep, he's got a good head for that. We looked through all your electronics together. He was as stunned as me at what we found in that 'cage'. I think he sees it as a challenge to get the camera system back up and running."

Larson has been sitting quietly, finishing his rabbit food plate, and calmly taking in all that has gone on. "Larson, you've had a big day already, go check on your cousins on the front porch, make sure they haven't started a corn battle or something stupid. Then take some down time. We all need some down time when we can get it."

"Okay, Pap," he says easily. "Pap, there's some contrails off to the east, have you noticed them?" He points over the mountain ridge. "They're small, but I been watchin' them."

We all turn, and look to where he is pointing. Sure enough, two thin contrails, running parallel, off to the east. Silence from us all as we digest this new development.

"Military planes, running a cap mission," states Ken.

I watch for a bit longer. "Gotta be. Hallelujah! Someone somewhere got a skycap mission going. Whoever hit us has been hit back, that's for sure, and whatever unit that is, it's still functional, it's put a protective cover over the coast. Something, somewhere is still operational." We all stare a few more moments at the sight, a bit of hope growing inside us all, at the thought that maybe normalcy can be restored.

I break the silence, "Come on, that air patrol won't help us out here in these mountains, let's go show you two what we got set up here."

Larson heads off to the old farmhouse as Janie, Ken, and I head in the house. First I show them the arms closet in the hallway of the kitchen with its heavy duty construction and lock. It usually only holds a fraction of what is actually on the premises. It's mostly empty now, these guns now being carried to protect the farmstead.

Then I take them downstairs to show them the hidden gun closet. It's not too fancy, not some five thousand dollar safe. It's a closet behind a closet in the basement. The front closet is a standard six foot wide closet with bi-fold doors. It holds your standard hunting gear, coats, pants, boots, vests, etc. If you push all the hunting gear aside, you see a paneled wall. In the upper left hand corner is a lock. You open it with the key hidden under the sink in the basement bath, and the wall opens to show a six foot wide four foot deep gun chest.

It is mostly your standard western Pennsylvania gun cabinet, three 30.06 scoped rifles, a 273 lever action with iron sights, a double barrel 12 gauge, two 16 gauge pumps, a couple of 22/410 squirrel guns and several pistols of various calibers. There are also drawers full of ammunition, cleaning kits, knives, etc. But there are three gems that Ken quickly notices. Two more AR15's, and a fifty caliber competition-quality long range target rifle.

"Holy crap, Mark!" exclaims Ken. "You got an arsenal here. That's a Barret fifty cal. You can reach out and touch someone with that!" I notice that his funk from the past events is moving away quickly. I hand him the weapon. He checks to make sure it is clear then runs it through his hands, checking it over in detail.

"That's my brother, John's rifle, 29 inch barrel, semi-automatic, with a ten round clip. I hope he makes it out here. In the mean time, I'll want you to put a few rounds down range with that." Ken sobers up a bit, and agrees to some range firing. These weapons are in addition to what is already being carried, Janie notes. I let them know I am expecting more of my family to show up, if they can get out of Pittsburgh.

Ken is looking over the drawers of ammunition. "There's more, Ken," I state as he is clearly calculating the ammunition stored here. I lock things up, and lead them to the basement bedroom, where Linc and Kim are staying. I unlock an underbed drawer, and roll it out. "I got as much money tied up in ammunition as I do in firearms." I roll open another drawer, revealing more ammunition and an unopened reloading kit. "John bought this, too. I don't even know how to use it, but if we need it we got it.'" Janie and Ken are both staring, open mouthed. "There's more." I show them the false back of another closet, and more ammunition. "It may look like a lot, but it isn't. We can hunt and defend the property for a while, but it will run out. And we all need to do some weapons training, and range shooting. I don't have a full inventory of what we have. Ken, I am hoping you will do that for us, and figure out what we can use for everyone to put a few rounds down range, so all adults, and grown children are comfortable with the weapons." Ken agrees, Janie is still open mouthed, but agrees as well. We decide that the next morning we will have weapons and range training. We can't have people carrying guns that they are not comfortable with, not able to maintain.

"The rest of the tour won't be as eye opening, but I think you will find it pleasing," I say as we head out the basement door, and over to the large garden shed. I show them the seed processing and storage area, and the drying racks. I briefly explain how we can replant everything we are growing this year, next spring. I let them know Becca and I have been doing this for several years, and that we can teach them how to do it; which crops to choose for seed stock, and how to harvest, and store the seeds. I show them the book we bought that explains it step by step for almost every crop we grow, from asparagus to zucchini.

I answer the questions they fire at me as best I can, as we head over to the old barn. There, I show them the secondary root cellar, already half full from this year's potatoes and onions that we have already harvested. There are also more perishable crops in there too, like squashes, peppers, and a few early cabbages, that will last longer in the cool, dry space. Ken notes the five gallon buckets with ten pound weights sitting on them. Sauerkraut presses, I explain briefly. Janie is not so impressed with the veggies but is happy about the potatoes. She wants to know if we have enough, if we know how to grow more. I answer her bluntly, no, we probably don't have enough potatoes, but yes we can, and will, grow more.

We pass the indoor portion of the pigpen. Bertha, our sow, is lolling in the shade, waiting for the next scraps to be thrown in for her. Her nine offspring are out roaming their acre of fenced-in land. They have almost grown to full size, close to two hundred pounds each. We would have been taking them in for sale in the next few weeks, keeping one for our own use. Now all will be kept for food, except for a few lucky ones that will be bred. In the next pen, with a smaller range, is Franklin, our stud boar. All our family knows we have been raising pigs for a few years. They all have been recipients of fresh bacon, pork and ham. I let them know we should keep two more sows, and another boar, to increase our pig stock. That means less meat now, but more meat in the future.

Next up are the larger cattle stalls. All four of our beef cattle are in the pasture, indifferent to the plight of us humans. Four heads will not go far, I tell them, remembering the boys herding the milk cows to town. On the other side of the barn basement is an area previously used for milk cows, now used as excess storage, literally filled with junk. I verbalize a plan to Ken and Janie, that we need to clean out all this junk and trade for milk cows, to start raising both cows and bulls. I task Janie with figuring this out, and tell her that she needs to talk with our neighbor, Thad, about what needs to be done. Our meat and potatoes girl quickly agrees to taking on the task.

We head up to the main level of the barn. There is a newer tractor, a tracked excavator, a big lawn tractor, and an older tractor sitting up here, along with various farm implements: some I use regularly, some have not been moved in fifty years. I task Ken to see what's running and what's not, to have Linc and Larson, Grace when available, to help.

We come to the more open storage area of the barn. It has been sectioned off. There is a forty foot by twenty foot area that has been walled off and turned in to my carpentry shop, What still works, I wonder? There are no electronics in a table saw or planer. How about my power saws and drills? That can be left for another day, I decide, despite my desire to check things out.

We come to another large sectioned off portion of the barn. It runs perpendicular to the shop area, across the back of the barn. It looks like a normal storage area, with eight foot sliding doors secured by a heavy hasp lock.

"This is our food storage locker. What I am about to show you, you cannot tell anyone else about. Not your kids, not your spouses, no one. If word gets out that there is food stored here, it will bring desperate people here, people willing to kill to feed their families. We want to help as many people as we can, but our best chance to help the most people is for us to survive the short term and become a food producing farm in the long term. We need to help other farmers as well, and we will all need more manual labor, and security to make it all happen. Those people that are willing to help in the long-term goals, we will help through the crisis as best we can. But we cannot make this farm a magnet for scavengers and anarchists.

"Promise me you will tell no one of our food stores." Both nod in agreement. "If your spouses, kids or anyone close asks, tell them we are struggling to get by, but we should make it to spring. God willing, we will make it. God put us all here for a reason. I believe that reason is to stay strong through this crisis, and become a beacon of hope, as our farm grows, as this whole farming community rebounds."

I unlock the hasp, and after a quick look around to make sure we are alone, I slide open the door, and usher my son-in-law and daughter-in-law into the food storage area. After turning on a light, I close and secure the door behind us.

***

In front of them is what looks to be a huge mish-mash of bins, cases, pallets, sealed buckets, and boxes. Some things are stacked very orderly, others items seem to just be boxes and bins piled up on each other. There are shelves packed full, and areas where boxes are stacked six feet high. One corner is so packed with boxes and crates that many items are inaccessible. They both look at me in surprise, shock, wonder. Questioning looks cross their faces.

"Mark, what are we looking at?" asks Ken. Janie is still staring at the horded food, agape with confusion.

"I'd like to tell you this is a storage sight of a well calculated system to provide food for thirty people for six or twelve months, whatever. No, you are looking at six years of food hoarding, buying things on the internet, stuff brought out by my brothers. Some brought here by Zach. It is a hodgepodge of longterm food. Let me show you around a bit.

"This whole shelf right here, these are prepackaged meals, survival food you hear about on the radio, just add water, and boil and you have a gourmet meal, shelf life of twenty-five years. We tried some, and they're actually pretty good. These stacks here are canned goods, soups, beans, veggies. Stated shelf life is only three years, but so long as the cans aren't damaged, they will last twenty years, too. Over here, in these sealed buckets, rices and beans, no seasoning, just rice and beans. But I have stacks of spices over there." I indicate another shelf. "Their shelf life is only three years, and some of them may have lost some flavor, but they won't actually have gone bad. We also have lots of fresh spices we grow every year, and many types of peppers, onions and garlic.

"Over there in that corner, that is the stuff that has been here the longest, that's more prepackaged food and canned goods. That stack of boxes over there, Janie, those are from Zach, those are boxes full of MRE's. I didn't ask where he got them, he just showed up with a truckload last year, said this would be a good place for them to be stored."

Janie looks at me a bit puzzled. "About a year ago he stacked about that many of those boxes in the basement. 'Just in case we need them' he said."

"What about flour, sugar, salt, coffee?" asks Ken

"Over on that shelf back there is instant coffee, it will last forever, but what is in the pantry is all we have of fresh coffee. There are also tins of sugar back there, and elsewhere. Next spring we'll tap the maples, and boil it down for more sugar and syrup. On the salt side, this is untested, but I figure we can boil rock salt, and then let it recrystalize. That should allow for the impurities to drop out and make it usable. Man has been purifying salt for centuries, so we'll figure it out.

"Flour doesn't store long term, so what's in the pantry is all we have. But wheat stores for years! There's five one-hundred pound sacks of whole grain wheat stored back there in those sacks, and it's two years old. I don't know how to grind it down to flour, but there is an actual millstone in front of the old farmhouse. We'll have to figure that out, too, but again, man has been doing it for thousands of years, we'll figure it out. There's also sacks of whole kernel corn, too. John brought all that here. It's supposed to be heirloom seed, not hybrid, so it can be planted and will produce seed."

"So Mark, your warehouse here, how much food do you think you have?" Janie asks.

"No idea." I reply. "It looks like a lot, but I still don't think it's enough. And the big problem is, I don't know what we have so I don't know how many people we can feed, and how long we can feed them."

"And that's part of the reason you're showing us this," says Ken. "You want us to organize and inventory this." He is smiling but shaking his head at the same time.

"Kenny, Kenny, Kenny, right to the point. It's a natural fit for you guys. Janie will be helping with the cooking, and you have that analytical mind of yours, that can sort this all out. Besides, you two got the most mouths to feed. Becca will help, too. She is antsy about knowing who we can help, how many we can bring into our little community."

Janie looks at me quizzically. "Zach brought out all the MRE's? Those stacks of family- sized cans look like his work too, so do a few other items I see around here. He knows all about this store room, doesn't he?" A tear starts to form in the corner of her eye. "That's why he was so insistent on us coming out here, he helped prep this for us!" She begins to cry, tears of sorrow, tears of respect, tears of joy. "He is such a good man," she manages to get out as she gives me a strong and deep hug. She steps back. "You and Becca raised a good man, thank you. Even though he is not here, he is still taking care of us."

"He is a good man, and he loves you and all the kids. Yes, he has seen this room, and all the other preparations. So have John and Paul. But we need to really know what we have. Over the next few weeks, we need to get this organized, and accounted for so we can figure out how many people we can support until next spring. Then we need to figure out how many we can support long term."

"I have to show you one more thing," I say as I lock up the doors, and lead them around the corner. "This may be a bigger problem. We need a way to store food. All those jars of jam we give you at Christmas, they are in short supply, the jars that is. We have a couple dozen cases, but that ain't much. From here on out, all food storage will be in sealed jars cooked off in a pressure cooker. These are going to be in high demand. We have to save every jar and lid like it is a precious commodity."

We head out of the barn, towards the old farmhouse. "You know about our gardens and fruit trees, the berry patches, we will need to nurture those, maybe plant some more fruit trees."

Becca, 30/30 slung over her shoulder, Glock on her hip, comes up from the new house. As she catches up to us she asks, "You showed them our food storage?" She turns to Ken and Janie, "He, we, have been gathering stuff for years, his brothers, too. I'm all for the self sufficient farming stuff, but all that food storage! I have no idea what's in there. And he and his brothers just kept bringing stuff out, saying they got some bargain here or there." She turns to Janie. "And Zach was in on it, too! He brought several truck loads of stuff out here that went into that storage room. I kept shaking my head then. Now I thank God." She grasps my arm gently. "Mark, all that food, it's still good, right, did everything look good to you?" She says stepping back, addressing us all.

"I'm impressed," states Ken. "I don't see any reason to question that food." Janie nods in agreement. "But we need an inventory," Ken says. "You're going to help us out with that, Mark says."

Becca gives me the look, then turns back to Ken. "It needs done, and Mr. Organization here will never get it done. Yes, I'll help organize it. Did Mark tell you we tried some of it, the prepackaged meals? It's really good." We banter back and forth, as we head up to the front porch of the old farmhouse.

***

As we come up to the front porch, Rusty and Blake are arguing over who had the highest level on the Halo video game, before the power went out. Janie quiets them, telling them it does not matter, that they need to concentrate on keeping watch, as they have been asked to do. Linc hollers from inside the house, asks us to come in, and see what he has set up.

Janie settles down on the porch with her boys as Becca, Ken, and I head in to see what Linc is so excited about. Linc has an old twenty-four inch Apple monitor set up on the large coffee table in the living room. He explains to us that he has four cameras working, and displaying on a twenty-inch screen in the new house, and has duplicated that display on this monitor here. He also has the wireless com link set up so whoever is in the farmhouse can ask for the picture displayed to be switched by whoever may be monitoring the screen in the new house. His wife is down there now, watching the kids. He runs us through a demo of moving from camera to camera with her running the controls. It is not Fort Knox, but it is impressive. He wants to have Rusty and Blake help him run a line out to the road. He already has everything lined up to do it. I tell him we will keep watch, and to get it done.

I sit back on the couch, looking at the monitor, as it flicks from scene to scene every three seconds. Becca settles in next to me. We see the lower pasture, three steers are grazing, and then it switches to the chicken coop area. Kim is down there with the young kids, feeding the chickens as the kids run about in an impromptu game of tag. The scene changes to a camera pointing from the new house, up past the barn to the old house. We see Linc and his crew heading towards the barn for the wire and tools to run new cameras out to the county road. The scene switches again to the view from the front porch. We see a vacant gravel road heading out past the lilac bushes, and through the fence line, rising between the cornfields, before it trails off to the unseen county road.

Thinking of all the people that have been thrown into chaos, and looking at the peace and security we have here, I am overwhelmed. "Wow, Becca! So much has happened in the past three days. But, look at us, we have the kids and grandkids here, we have found two good people we were able to help, and we have helped the town move towards some kind of stability. All the preparations we have made over the years, they are working. God has truly blessed us."

"He has, Mark, he has. I just pray for Mellonie and Brad. And Zach, too, what is he going through? What do they have him doing? And we don't know about your family. Do you think they will be able to make it out here? So much has happened, so much has changed. But God put us in a good position, Mark, and I pray that we can follow the path he wants us to follow."

"I worry about all that, too, baby doll. I'm sure that Zach's reserve unit could only put a skeleton crew together. I am not sure what they will be able to do and, more importantly, where their orders will come from. Mellonie and Brad are in a good place. Game is plentiful in those mountains, and they have good neighbors. Paul and John, and their wives, that's more of a concern to me. How are they going to make it fifty miles from Pittsburgh to here? We talked about it, but no solid plans were made."

I feel my eyelids getting heavy, it's been a long few days. I doze off on the couch, leaving my worries in God's hands. I silently pray that we have been righteous, that we all have done the right thing in his eyes.

Chapter 27 Wagerlys' Compound, September 13, 2018

Frank is not in a good mood. Things aren't going as planned. It is the third morning after the power went out, and his plans of domination are bogging down. He has a large group, over fifty people now, some camped out in tents, some taking shelter in the run down out buildings. He has been able to feed them, thanks to the tribute he is getting from some local farmers, whose women he has captive. And he has enough booze and drugs to keep his thugs motivated.

But some hard headed vigilantes from the local towns are screwing with his plans. Two of his boys getting killed took a toll on him, and left a gap in dependable leadership. The roadblocks that have been set up are better than he ever thought they would be. Instead of owning the roads, they have to skirt around on the back roads to get anywhere. Even the local farmer boys have set up positions to stop anyone from coming onto their farms. He lost two guys just to get one cow!

It is time to start some extreme violence, he thinks. Time to turn things to the way he thinks things should be run. But he needs information, he needs to know what the locals have set up. He spends the day sending out scout patrols, two trucks with serious fire power, and a couple of bikes as cavalry. They are to run at the roadblocks, see what resistance they face. They are to shoot things up as best they can, put fear into the townsfolk. They are to do the same at the farms, run up and shoot, see what happens, find the weak spots. Any farms that are weak, his guys are to pillage, bring back food and women, booze, if they have it, anything else his guys find as useful. Anything they see on the roads, they are to eye it up before committing to violence. He doesn't want to see losses like happened yesterday. That will be his plan for the day. He smiles at the havoc he is about to unleash.

Chapter 28 Wagerlys' Compound, September 14, 2018

Frank Wagerly is in a much better mood today. He stayed away from the wine, and stuck to the whiskey and beer, no raging hangover. A group from his primary suppliers in Pittsburgh has shown up, increasing the numbers of his small army. There was an incident the night before, when a few of the women they had grabbed revolted. But that had been taken care of. His patrols have brought back food and good information. He knows where there are weak farms. He knows the layout of the town's barricades. And, most importantly, he is finding information on the vigilante who had murdered his sons; a guy named Mark, who has a farm outside Central City.

He is about to reveal his plans to his two remaining sons and some trusted lieutenants when he hears some farm trucks roll up outside. He smiles, thinking he has more recruits. He turns and heads out to see what's up. He walks outside only to see his people scrambling, ducking for cover, grabbing firearms. He looks out the farm road leading to his makeshift roadblock, and sees three unfamiliar trucks. Several armed people exit the trucks, and bear arms in a ready stance. These are not new recruits to his kingdom.

A large man he recognizes as the fire chief from Hooversville steps out, He has a semiautomatic rifle held across his chest. He hollers for Frank to come out, to give himself up, and to stop his ravaging of the countryside. He begins to say something about taking care of everyone there, but his voice is drowned out as Hairy, in a strategic position in the barn loft, unleashes with his 30 cal machine gun. Others in Frank's group start firing, too. Frank yells encouragement to Hairy, and everyone else, to kill the bastards intruding on their property.

The intruders make an attempt to regroup. Their leader is torn up in the initial blast. The first truck in line has been riddled with bullet holes. Quickly, the two trucks behind hit reverse and get out of the fire zone. Fire continues on the retreating trucks until they drop over a rise, and are out of sight. Revving engines can be heard as they try to turn around in the narrow lane and flee the killing zone.

Frank looks up to the hayloft, and receives a thumbs up from his friend, Hairy. Hairy hollers at him, "Ain't no pussy townsfolk gonna mess with us, boss!" Frank waves for Hairy to come down, and they both walk out to survey the carnage. A follower points out the fire chief as the one who killed Frank's nephew. There are three other people dead at the scene. Frank smiles.

"This will let them know we mean business. You can't roll up on Frank Wagerly and not pay for it." He lets out in a tirade of cuss words about how the towns and farmers will pay. He gathers his men to let them know his plans to start more chaos. They devise a plan on how to deliver a gruesome message to Hooversville.

Frank has more than just a few military grade machine guns, he has lots of stuff that will show the townsfolk and farmers that he means business. He orders two trucks and ten men, along with two bikes as scouts, to go to a local farm. He knows they have pigs. "Kill everyone, bring back some pigs. If they have women, bring them back, too. Let's have a pig roast!" He shouts. He is met by cheers. He orders people around. "Get a fire pit going, get another keg tapped, let's get a party going here, you sluggards!"

Hairy issues a few more orders, makes sure the 30 cal gets cleaned and oiled, sets up some scouts, and sets a better roadblock. Hairy suppresses his thoughts about Frank. He makes sure the guys he brought in are seeing to getting things more secure.

Chapter 29 Farmstead, Day 4, September 14, 2018

It is quiet. It is dark. I look at my bedside clock, and it is dark, too. My long sleep has not changed anything. I look over at my wife, and thank God for all the blessings in my life. Reality comes rushing in, and I think of the many Bible verses that extol us to praise the Lord, even in our times of trouble. When we are surrounded by a storm, as the apostles were, Jesus walked on water, and calmed the storms, calmed the waters. I think about it a bit, and the storms have been calmed. My children and grandchildren, those that I could help, they are all here with me. We are all safe. We have food, water, and shelter. A storm is raging about us, but here we have a calm in the storm, just as Jesus provided on the Sea of Galilee. I take comfort in that thought as I hear a rooster start to crow.

As I quietly get to the kitchen and methodically begin to make coffee, I ponder the day before. I fell asleep exhausted, on the couch in the old farmhouse. I awoke in my own bed. I smile at the thought of how I got there, how blessed I am to have such great kids. I set the percolator on a high heat, and my mind starts to wander about what we have, and how long it will last. How long will the propane tank last? It's half empty I'm sure. Where can we get a replacement? What do we do when there is no more propane? Can we convert this stove to a wood stove?

The rooster crows again. I see the first peeks of dawn come over the ridge. The sight is beautiful; the deep pinks, the dark purples, and the vibrant oranges spreading across the eastern sky. No man can paint such a beautiful scene. I do some kitchen clean up as the coffee begins to percolate. After pouring a cup for myself, I pour the rest of the coffee into a thermos carafe, and walk out to the eastward facing porch.

I sit down and enjoy my fresh cup of coffee, lighting up a cigarette, enjoying the nicotine jolt. My mind wants to wander to things I should worry about. I refuse to go there, willing my mind to enjoy the moment of peace. The sky lightens to shades of dark blue and brilliant oranges. A hoot owl is heard in the distance, giving his last call of the night. A steer moos lowly as the tit mouses and chickadees get active at the bird feeder. Not to be outdone, two blue jays show up and begin fighting and cawing over the few berries left on the elderberry tree. It is a good morning at the farmstead, I smile.

I take a few moments to pray. To thank God for helping us to get to where we are, to pray for those in distress, to pray for my family who arr not here, to pray for those who would bring evil upon this land, that He may change their hearts,. To pray that God will guide us in the days to come.

A loud shrill shriek in the distance disturbs my time with God. I look about, recalling the noise: a bobcat or coyote, getting a kill, a rabbit looking for a tender green shoot is now food for a higher predator. The circle of life continues in nature, even when man's world has been turned upside down.

I hear the clanking of a coffee mug, and the shuffling of feet. Linc soon appears at the door. He comes out and joins me on the porch.

"Good morning," I say quietly. "Early riser?" I ask.

"Good morning to you, and no, not usually. But, I went to bed shortly after sunset, so I guess the new normal is to get up at sunrise," he responds.

"Well, if you look right over there, between those two big willows down by the pond, you will see the sun rise over the ridge in just a few minutes. So technically, you woke up at dawn, not sunrise. But I'll give a city slicker like you a break." I turn and smile at him. He nods and smiles back.

We sit quietly on the porch for several minutes. But nature is not quiet. The blue jays continue their bickering, several pairs of cardinals sing their distinctive chirp as they warily make their way to the bird feeder. The ducks have begun to get noisy, and the hens are starting to cluck. Several more low moos come from the pasture as the steers begin foraging.

The sounds of a normal morning in the country surround us. I see a smile emerge on Linc's face. Too quickly it is replaced by sternness. "I can't believe I'm sitting here watching the sun rise, and actually enjoying it, but then I think of the chaos we saw. Two days ago we gunned down five people to save our lives. Now I'm sitting here, five hundred miles from home, and I feel like I am at home. I'm sorry, Mark, but I can't put my arms around it."

"If it's any consolation, Linc, I can't either. One moment, I am praising the Lord for all his blessings, the next moment I am praying that He will touch the hearts of those who want to kill us. And right now, with these meth head savages running around, there is a lot of killing going on. Yet, I pray for those doing the killing. That they may turn from the path they are on. And I know chaos is overtaking the entire country, if not the entire world. Yet we sit here and enjoy the beauty of this place that God has blessed us with and plan to not only survive but thrive, and to also help others survive, and thrive too.

"Linc, its all part of a plan. Not necessarily my plan, nor my family's plan, but God's plan.

I don't know why these attacks occurred. I don't know why God is allowing chaos, and anarchy to consume this country. Maybe it's part of some great reset, a test of the faithful through which we will all emerge stronger and better people, a kinder and more loving people, a harder working more self reliant people. Heck, Linc, when this all started, I thought it was going to be the Rapture, when God calls those who believe in him home. But we're all still here, struggling to make sense of it, struggling to survive. I can't make any sense of it, but I have to trust in God, he has a plan."

"You have great faith in God," Linc says. "I see it in your actions, I hear it in your words. You're not the hypocrite that many of my Christian friends sometimes seem to be. You smoke, and you have shared your bourbon with me, which some would say makes you a sinner, and therefore a hypocrite. But you have a peace in your heart that I can't fathom.

'You go out of your way to help people, setting out cases of water on the road for strangers, trying to talk peace with the bandits on the road, offering rides to strangers, helping the town folk work things out. I know there is a violence in you to protect your family from harm, but that is held deep down. You show kindness, and respect, even love to total strangers. I hope someday to have that same peace you have, that love for God and for my fellow man: a true sense of why God put me here, that great sense of purpose that I see in you." He pauses and sips his coffee. "I'm sorry, Mark, I didn't mean to ramble on like this, but I think I will enjoy having coffee in the morning with you." We sit together quietly for a few moments. "I need to go check on Kim." He states. Before I can respond, he heads back in the house.

Here is a man I need to reach out to. I need to find the right words, the guidance he needs to build a stronger relationship with God. I say a short prayer that God will give me those words.

***

As the farmyard sounds grow louder, I rise to make sure people are getting up to take care of the chores. Becca begins to start making bacon and eggs for breakfast as I head up to the old farmhouse to see how things are up there. Ken and Larson are sitting watch on the front porch, Ken watching the sunrise while still keeping an eye on the lane, Larson watching the laptop display of our remote cameras. I have the next watch with Blake. Ken goes to roust him, and he soon joins me, a bit grumpy, and sleepy-eyed. Larson and Ken head off for some breakfast with the rest of the household.

An hour later, Becca shows up with two plates of cold eggs and some bacon. We both hungrily chow it down. Becca and I discuss what needs to be done for the day. We have an abundance of tomatoes that need to be stewed and canned. Same with the green beans and sweet corn, all of which needs blanched and canned. This will keep the women and kids busy all day. The camera system is good, but I want a better roadblock on the lane, in front of the old farmhouse, at the property line. I also tell her of another project I want to get started. I get glares from her on this project. She says I need to talk to the kids first, meaning our adult children. She doesn't want them thinking they are living in a fortress. We agree that we need to talk it over with Ken, Britt and Janie before I start this new project.

Everyone gets about their chores as the day moves on. We tow my 2012 Dodge up and place it across the opening in the fence at the property line. We rig up a quick tow system with the lawn tractor so it can be moved easily, if needed. Beyond the fence is my neighbors leased cornfield, which the farmer, Thad, also maintains. The cornfield helps keep us hidden, but can also hide anyone encroaching on the farmstead. We decide that it must be harvested, and that we need to talk with Thad about getting that done soon, and maybe trading for the crops to help feed our livestock. We have an agreement with Thad that we get enough corn from our acreage to feed our beef cows, and two pigs, but since we want to expand our livestock, we will need more feed.

I have Rusty and Janie walk with me to the neighbor's house. It has been lifeless for three days, but we feel we should check in, before we proceed with our plan. Our neighbors are empty nesters. He is in consulting and is often in DC or other cities, and she is a nurse at Windber Hospital. The house is still dark. No one answers after repeated knocking at the doors. We say a brief prayer, that the Lord will protect them. We decide to have Thad harvest the corn as soon as he can.

When we get back to the old farmhouse, lunch is being served. We have bread for tuna sandwiches, Britt made two loaves of bread from scratch. After we have eaten, I pull Britt, Ken, and Janie aside with Becca. I share my concerns with them that if some meth heads decide to roll down the lane, and shoot up the house, we could be devastated. A few years back, my brother John found a pallet of military grade sandbags for cheap, and had them shipped here. My proposal is to start filling those sandbags, and fortifying the front wall of the farmhouse. I refrain from using the phrase fighting positions, but the idea has been put forward. The initial goal would be to secure the areas around the front facing windows, so that we could fire at anyone coming down the road from a safe position. I also stress that this will make anyone in those rooms mainly them, and their children, more secure if we get assaulted. The conversation that follows goes in favor of fortifying the farmhouse, and any place else that needs to be made secure. I am surprised, and so is Becca. But what we are doing will make everyone safer, and we all have seen the savages' ability to attack ruthlessly.

The sandbag project begins almost immediately. Britt and Janie both want to be involved because it is their living space that is being protected, their families that are being made more secure. That leaves Becca and Kim with the kids and the canning.

The biggest problem with this project is sand; we don't have any. We have a short term solution to the problem; our ever-present pile of 2A limestone gravel. That's a large pile of gravel that we always keep on hand for road repairs and other uses.

We set the older boys to filling sand bags, and hook up the bike trailer to the older tractor for hauling the filled bags up to the farmhouse. Ken, Britt, and Janie take charge of placing the sandbags. Linc and I begin to search for a good substitute once the gravel is gone.

We put the field dirt as a backup plan. It is very close to the farmhouse, but not a good option. We choose to go down by the stream on the lower edge of the property. Here we locate good sand and gravel, as I expected, and as Linc said we would. But it is far away from where we need it.

We head back up to the barn to fire up the Kubota. It is an older model with all hydraulic controls and a simple diesel engine, no electronics. As we head up to the barn I find out Linc can run the machine, and I gladly delegate that job to him. He takes the tracked backhoe down the pasture road to the closet point to the stream. I follow in the old John Deere with the front end bucket. From the end of the trail, it takes Linc about fifteen minutes to move some small trees and brush to get to where a good riffle empties into a pool, about twenty yards long, and fifteen feet wide. It is one of my favorite trout holes.

As we decide where best to situate the machines, and drop the sand, we talk about all the permits we would need to do this five days ago. The environmental impact studies, creating a system to divert the water around our dig site, the run off filters and the inspections. We laugh as we both concur that our request to dig gravel from the stream would have been denied after two years litigation, and thousands of dollars in fees.

I wait as he digs out a couple of scoops, just where the riffle ends. It is good pebbly sand. There are some bigger rocks, but most of it will work just fine. I give him my com set and leave him to his task.

It is mid-afternoon, and the skies are clouding over. It has been hot and dry for several days but I feel the humidity rising. I can tell we'll be in for a good storm in a few hours. Looking to the west, thick dark clouds are showing the signs of a storm front approaching.

I check on the ladies, and they are starting to wrap up the last batch of canned tomatoes for the day. Then they are going to clean up, and get ready to make dinner. Becca brings up that she doesn't think we should can as much corn or beans, maybe a few other vegetables as well. We should use most of them for seed. That way we will have enough seed set aside for planting next year's crops, and be able to give away or trade seeds as well. We both agree that we need to help people get their own crops going next year. She points out that we should have plenty of food from our storeroom for this year, but our ability to grow more, everyone's ability to grow more, needs to be the priority. I agree with her, but we need to get the inventory going. She says she'll get started on that with Ken and Janie as soon as the "damned sandbag project'" is done. I know it disturbs her to think that we need that kind of protection; that her kids, and grandkids need to sleep in a fortified house. But I also know she understands the need.

***

Up at the farmhouse I find the entire crew resting in the shade of the porch, drinking water, and trying to cool off. "What, are we all getting ready for a game of spades?" I ask jokingly, as I look around.

"We've been working our butts off, Pap," responds Larson as he throws a sweat soaked t-shirt my way.

"I can see that!" They have stacked sandbags eight feet along each side of the porch stairs to the top of the railing, forty two inches high. That's over fifty sandbags. It looks good, well stacked with a perpendicular wall started at the steps and at about six feet from the steps on each side.

As I am surveying the progress, Janie chimes in. "There's more than that upstairs. You should go take a look." I head inside. Grace is sitting on the couch talking to Linc on the com, and watching the camera display. "Hi, Pap!" He says brightly.

"Feeling better I see. You got clearance from your mom for this duty?"

"I nagged her till she let me. I'm good, the arm is feeling better, and no redness so it's okay," he responds. "I gotta keep an eye on these cameras, and make sure Linc is okay, Pap." He says, dismissing me so that he can attend to his duties. I shake my head, smiling at his composure and fortitude.

Upstairs the women have the bags stacked ten feet along the front wall and six feet along the side wall in both front bedrooms, three feet high. The obvious intent is to protect anyone sleeping in the beds, but one front window in each room is protected. And soon, the side windows and the other front windows will be protected, too.

"You all filled and moved about two hundred sandbags! That's impressive!" I exclaim as I walk back out to the front porch. "But that's got to be putting us close to being out of gravel."

Ken points at the trailer with maybe a ton of gravel on it. "That's the last of the gravel there, about fifty more sandbags. We're going to use them all upstairs."

"I'm good with that. I'm glad you fortified the porch positions. And the rooms upstairs look good, too. Linc is digging good gravel and sand out of the creek, but it may take a day or two to get it moved up here. But what you all got done, that's a good start, it's more than a good start. Now, I hate to say this, but you need to rehearse with the young ones in getting out of bed and getting into the safe areas. You all need to do it too, so you know who can help defend the house, and how much room you have to move around."

That comment gets nods from all of them, but a bit of a glare from Britt. It's the same look I get from Becca when I say something that she doesn't like. "Ken, you see any structural issues with all this extra weight?"

"I'm a little concerned, but with this old chestnut framing, it's really not an issue. That old wood gets as hard and strong as steel. I don't think we have to worry about it." He looks to the west, to the coming front. "I'm more worried abou that right now we're going to get rained on pretty good in an hour or two. We're going to finish up with the gravel we got, then start to wrap things up."

"Sounds good to me. Then we should do a few quick drills, so everyone knows where to go if these meth heads come rolling in here. Ya'll done a great job, especially you boys," I say, looking at the three teens on the porch. "Wasn't this a lot more fun than playing Halo3 all afternoon?"

I get heckled and booed as I walk down the steps and out the drive to look at the house from our driveway. It looks good. Because of the railings, the porch sandbags are hardly noticed. Everything else looks like a normal old farmhouse.

Two hours later we are back at the new house; spread out from the porch, through the great room, and into the kitchen. Kim and Becca are getting dinner together. Linc and Larson are standing guard at the farmhouse with Grace still manning the monitors and com system. The rest of us are in various states of relaxation after a hard day's work. The storm that had been threatening all day has finally broken, starting in spits with distant rumbles of thunder, and lightning flashing across the sky. I'm on the front porch with a few others. "These are God's fireworks," I comment, as I take a sip of one of the few beers left. A loud rumbling thunderclap follows the lightning bolt, as the rain begins to come down in sheets.

"What's that ringing I hear?" asks Blake. We all freeze. The school bell is ringing, loud and constant. We have visitors, unknown visitors. There is panic, and confusion. Ken has already grabbed his AR15, and is sprinting towards the farmhouse.

I look around for my weapon. Leaning next to the front door, I think. And there it is. I holler into the house. "The alarm is ringing! You all stay here, we're going to check it out." I see Janie has already grabbed her weapon, and is heading out the door. I run with her towards the farmhouse and the clanging bell.

Chapter 30 Day 4 Herc to Central City, September 14, 2018

Herc is awake as the sun comes up. Leesa and John Jr. are sleeping on the adjoining cot. He ponders what has happened over the past few days. The long walk home, fighting the fires the next day, then losing his Mom and brother. Yesterday they had traveled here, to Benson Borough. He looks around, he has his weapons, and personal belongings with him, and his family. He is in a church basement with a few dozen other people. The people here have treated him well, he is happy to be safe, and with his family, what family he has left..

He heads towards what he can see is the kitchen, dodging the many other cots with other refugees still sleeping. He greets an elderly woman and her young helper with a smile, and offers to help getting the coffee and breakfast going. The woman greets him warmly. She is a bit surprised at his eagerness to help because most who have come through their aid station expect to get help, but don't offer to give help.

He helps get the coffee brewing, and works the scrambled eggs for forty people. He finds time to step out for a smoke. After he piles scrambled eggs into the large warmer pan, he heads over to where Leesa and young John are starting to stir from a restless night's sleep. They all go through the line together and get a good breakfast. Before they begin to eat, they stop and share a short blessing, thanking God for the food before them. Herc thinks about how many times they have said the same grace automatically. This time it has way more meaning.

As they are eating, a tall lean farm boy with cropped hair comes up and kneels beside Herc. "Frankie says you'll help run guard on a run to Hooversville." He glances at Leesa and John Jr. "They comin' with you?"

Herc looks at the young man. He looks at his family. He thinks of his momma and brother. It only took a minute of him being off guard to lose his momma and brother. Leesa and John Jr. will go wherever he goes. "They ain't leavin' my sight...so, yeah, they go with me."

"Okay. We'll be pulling out soon, but you got to come with me so we can set up a protocol with the other trucks" says Brush Cut.

Herc looks him over, thinks about what he has said. "I'm all in," he states. "But I got a lawn tractor with a trailer parked outside. All our stuff is there, everything, all our food and clothes. I'll leave the lawn tractor and trailer, but I need to take our stuff, as much as we can."

"We'll make room for it, get organized so it's easy to move and haul." Brush Cut turns and tells Leesa where the convoy will be meeting up. Herc heads off with his new comrade to find three pickup trucks and six other men, armed as well as he is. The one in charge is Frankie, from the day before.

"Okay guys, this shit sucks. We got Jimmy, who needs to get home, Manda needs to check in on her momma, Herc and his family need safe passage, and we just need to take back this road from the junkies. We know at least twenty people have been killed between here and Hooversville in the last few days. We know most of them have been stragglers from the Flight 93 Memorial, but some of them have been our friends, people we know, our neighbors.

"We also know that one of us locals knocked some of them down, fought back. That sent them back up to the Route 30 area, as best we know. But we will be the first coordinated effort to run through to Hooversville since the power went out." Frankie continues on, letting them know who will be in which trucks, where to look out, etc. Frankie served in Iraq it turns out. This is not new to him. Each man has an assignment, and Frankie makes sure everyone knows what to do if they encounter trouble. At ten o'clock the convoy rolls out.

Herc sits in the front corner of the bed of an old farm truck, first truck in the convoy. Leesa lays next to him in the bed of the truck with two donated duffels full of their last precious possessions. Herc sees the bloated dead bodies at the first bridge. He sees other dead bodies along the road, and at some houses and farms. He sees a few barricaded homes with frightened kids and dads behind makeshift walls. They come into Hooversville thirty minutes later, after clearing their roadblock. Hugs are shared as people from two nearby communities are reunited. But there is a pall of gloom in the air.

He sees Frankie head off to what looks like some kind of command post with a lot of armed guys milling about, some arguing, some trying to calm things down. A state of confusion and panic seems to prevail.

An older man, maybe mid-fifties' hollers for everyone to quiet down so a young man, bandaged, but still bleeding, can tell what happened.

"Yeah, they was ready for us when we rolled up!" says the young man. "They opened up on us before we had a chance. They had some serious firepower. Chief Speigle had us stop short of a small barricade. He hollered for Frank Wagerly to come out, that the anarchy was going to stop, and it was going to stop now. Nothing happened, but we saw a few guys moving here and there. Then wham! They opened up on us heavy! They got an old M60 or something. We got ripped apart. We got in some return fire, but us in the two trail trucks, we had to git. We couldn't try to get the Chief, and the three with him; they got ripped down bad. We had to git. You see how bad we got shot up." In his words they all can feel his shame in leaving behind their friends, their comrades, and leader.

Herc listens further to the group and the heated conversation that rages back and forth among the men and a few women. It turns out the town sent a posse to the compound of the junkies and meth heads they think are causing all the mayhem. It was led by their fire chief, a Gulf War vet, who had stepped up as a leader. Twelve men and four women had gone out in three farm trucks. Two farm trucks, nine men and three women returned. They all said getting the fallen would have been suicide. The compound had over fifty people and all were well armed. The firepower was over whelming.

It becomes apparent that no one is in charge. Their leader had been Fire Chief Speigle, but he is now dead or captured. Now they all argue amongst themselves. Some want to negotiate a truce, some want to hunker down and wait for help, a few want to retaliate. Others say you can't negotiate with killers and rapists. Still others note that no help has come for those at the Flight 93 Memorial, so why would they come to help their little town. Most say retaliation won't work since they have already lost some of their best men. No one can agree on anything.

Finally, an old coot, wiry with steely gray eyes, a hard life written on every wrinkle in his face, stands and calls for attention. He is ignored. He speaks louder and a few turn to listen, but the general confusion continues around him. Frankie recognizes the face of the old coot from the VFW, and calls for calm, but he is also ignored. He pulls his shotgun, and fires three shots in the air. The crowd goes silent.

"The commander wants to speak!" Frankie states firmly. Most in the small town think the 'commander' is just a few loose nuts away from the looney farm. Frankie and many of the other vets know better since they have talked with him at the VFW, the way only vets can talk. The commander served in Vietnam, three tours from 1967 to 1970. One of the original Special Forces, he earned a Silver Star, two Bronze Stars, and three Purple Hearts. He was demoted and discharged on trumped up charges for doing his job, the job the United States Army trained him to do. Although he had been through some rough times, the commander had a good head on his shoulders.

With a high and whiney voice, the commander speaks out. "Ya'll arguin' ain't gonna get shit done, and you ain't got time to be arguing. If I'm the Wagerly's, I'm already comin' down the road for ya. I'll show up on your doorstep as soon as possible. There's only four roads into town. Get 'em manned up now. Someone take charge of that, and get moving. Quit yer pissin' about, and get it done. And don't expect no one to be helping you, go find help. These folks got here from Hollsopple, they'll help you. Unite with the other towns, Central City, Jerome. One of ya needs to step up and start making sure ya'll can communicate. And if you go runnin' off half-cocked after those bastards without a plan, you'll get killed, just like Chief Speigle. Scout, probe, set up a plan. Be smarter than them. Go get Jerry to figure this out, or one of the other vets. If you ask for their help, they'll help. It's in their blood." He pulls a flask from his hip pocket, and takes a short draw. His eyes grow weary for a minute, then brighten again. "We is all in a world of deep shit. If you ain't smart, it will go bad. Be smart." The commander sits back down and takes another draw from his flask. He is done with what he had to say. But what he had to say has sunk in with enough men who know his caliber.

An Army Reserve Staff Sergeant who had been helping with the roadblocks steps forward to take charge of making sure all the roadblocks are manned. Frankie steps up to continue making sure the roads are open between Hooversville and Hollsopple, and that they coordinate efforts. Another man, a trucker, no military experience, says he'll make sure to open things up to Central City. Two pastors step forward to say they will coordinate refugee efforts and relief for locals in need. Some order starts to take place, with people migrating to where they think they can help.

The beginning of orderliness is broken by gunfire. A few random shots at first, then heavy fire, and a few explosions followed by long strings of automatic ans semi automatic gunfire. There is panic for a moment. Some men pick up their arms, and start heading towards the gunfire. A few run from the gunfire or take cover. The commander and those that stepped up to lead take note. They know who to have on the frontline and who to have as helpers. Before anyone can get moving, the area goes quiet again, and the gunfire ceases.

Only the Staff Sergeant's loud bellowing stops the rush towards where the gunshots had rung out. He quickly gathers five men to send off towards the roadblock where the firefight just took place. He sends three men to each of the other three roadblocks, giving them instructions for how to set things up, and to be on high alert. He lets each of them know he will be by to check on things. Frankie starts to organize his return convoy, gathering information, and letting people know of a safe ride to Davidsville. The trucker starts recruiting farm truck drivers for a heavily armed move to Central City. His mom and brother live up that way, so he has added incentive to get there.

The wiry gray-eyed commander looks around at the more orderly direction that the agitated mob has taken. He catches the eye of the Staff Sergeant and gives him a nod, which puffs up the sergeant, as he continues to organize roadblock deployments. The two pastors are heading off with a dozen eager helpers. But the commander knows bad news is coming from the roadblock, where the short raid just occurred.

***

Shortly later, an older teen, who had headed off with the five reinforcements, comes sprinting back. He is out of breath, and a little sickly looking, like he has just thrown up. "Sergeant! You gotta come see this! It's bad! They, they,,,," he stutters. He turns and vomits again, but there is nothing inside him, he dry heaves several times. Several people rush to help him, consoling him, trying to find out what he has to say. The sergeant kneels down next to him and offers him some water.

"It's okay, son, tell me what you saw," he offers kindly.

"They cut his head off!" the teen blurts out. "And they attached a note." He dry heaves more. "They cut his freakin' head off!" he begins to sob. "They cut his head off," he says again, slowly, angrily. "And they left a note."

The sergeant points to three able men, including Herc, and tells them to follow him as he quickly makes his way to the roadblock that was attacked. No one hesitates as they grab their weapons, and run towards the site of the attack.

They arrive on the scene minutes later. Three people are being bandaged up, to be taken back to town for treatment. One is badly injured. Herc figures he will bleed out before he can get help. The scene at the roadblock is devastating. The two explosions have thrown cars off to the side. If the attackers had wanted to, they could have driven through easily. Three more guards at the roadblock have injuries, but refuse to leave their posts. They are bleeding from small wounds and gashes that have been patched up with shirtsleeves and bandanas, whatever was available. Herc is struck numb by the devastation and gore before him. Instinctively he jumps into the line, standing watch behind a twisted old Pontiac; he doesn't have first aid skills, but he does have weapons skills.

He surveys the scene in front of him. The road heads out of town, turning to the right, past a few houses, with the headwaters of the Stoneycreek River below them. To the left of the road, the hillside soars steeply for several hundred feet. Down by the river are some well kept gardens. He sees a rabbit scurry into a row of late season lettuce. Two blue jays hoot and cackle, as they fight each other over a mulberry tree. The river, maybe twenty feet wide at this point, slowly meanders by, several deep pools surely swimming with trout and bluegills.

But Herc's attention is drawn to the road where two men are inspecting a lifeless body, as a third man looks around intently as their scout. The body is headless. Herc turns, and pukes, what remains of the good breakfast he helped prepare ends up on the road beside him. He wipes his eyes, and again looks at the dead body about fifty feet in front of the road block. Indeed, there is visibly seen a note pinned to the dead man's chest.

Herc watches as a husky woman in a civilian medic's uniform runs out with a stretcher. She has the two men help her load the gruesome cargo, and they all head back to the safety of the roadblock. A young man with a farm tractor already has a few cars in position to fill the gap that the renegades had blown out.

Herc keeps his eyes down road, he knows that is his job right now, but he can't help but overhear the conversation of the medic and the sergeant.

The medic hurries off to look after the injured. The sergeant reads the note aloud to a few close by civilians.

"I am king now. Do not send your heroes after me. This will be their fate. As king, I will demand tribute. Be prepared to pay heavily. You and your rules mocked me and jailed me, now is my time. There are no more rules, I will make my own rules. This man killed my nephew. Your people killed two of my sons. I will exact revenge. There will be no tribute for those who killed my sons. Their fate, and those that help them, is death. I have gold and food for anyone who helps me put their heads on a pike."

The sergeant looks up and is pissed. He begins to crumple the paper, to discard it, but one of the civilians stops him. "Everyone needs to see this, we have to take it back to town." The sergeant nods to her as he straightens the note. His stare is distant as he looks down the road heading out of town. He barks some orders to get the roadblock more secure with more vehicles and flankers up on the hillside. He turns, with a look of disgust on his face as he heads back towards town with the note in his hand.

Herc listens to all this as he stands guard at the roadblock. He wants to let the sergeant know he is detailed to a convoy for Central City, but he doesn't want to upset matters, so he stands his position. An old high lift rolls up with a big new Yukon in tow. They quickly maneuver it into position in the roadblock, and the machine operator heads off for another useless vehicle. Herc notes how funny it is that fifty thousand dollar cars are used for a roadblock, and thirty year old rusted farm trucks are worth their weight in gold. He thinks of Leesa and John Jr., and is content that they are safe back at the church refugee shelter. But he has to figure out how to get back there for the convoy without leaving his position open.

Several hours later, the sergeant comes back, looking weary from the day's events, even though it is not yet mid-afternoon. As the sergeant passes, Herc waves him down. "I was at the meeting this morning when this all went down. Ya'll picked me to help man the roadblock. But ya'll also picked me to help the trucker run a convoy to Central City. I'll stay here as long as you need me here, but the trucker guy, he may be lookin' for me, ya know?"

The sergeant stops and looks Herc over. "Yeah, I remember you, you rode guard on the convoy in from Davidsville. Okay. Hey John!" he hollers at the guy organizing things at this roadblock. "Find someone to spell this man, he needs to ride convoy support to Central City." A young man, still in his teens, shouldering a 30.06, comes over and relieves Herc. Herc points out his hide spot and the best fields of fire to the young man, who is impressed, and a little slack jawed as the gravity of the responsibility he has been given begins to sink in. This is no video game. That is real blood on the road, people he knows are really dead, no game reset. Herc gives the teenager words of encouragement before heading back to town.

When he gets to the church where his family is, he sees the pastor and a few men in an animated discussion. There is no anger that he can hear, more frustration. "We got to get word to the guy somehow," one man says.

"His name was Mark, and he lives in Central City," states a woman. "I talked with him and his family when they passed through for some refreshments."

"That's not much to go on, but we gotta let him know, him and his family are in the cross hairs of this thug," states another man. "I thought he said he had a farm outside of town. And he had lots of kids and grandkids, that van and trailer was really loaded down."

Herc stops to listen. He interjects into the discussion. "Don't mean to be eavesdroppin', but this guy you're talkin' about, did he run a construction company?" He is met with a few puzzled looks. "Was he mid-fifties, short gray beard, and dirty blond hair? Talked about God, and said everything would be okay?"

"Yeah!" says the woman, "He said a short prayer with me. I was really frazzled, it calmed me down. Do your know him?"

"Mark? Mark Mays? Knowed him for fifteen years, I work for him!" Herc says proudly. "He in trouble? I'm tryin' to get out to his place, I can pass on the word."

They all look at him a little shocked. He has gone three days with no change of clothes, no shower, he has fought fires, fought bandits, killed people. He looks a little rough. Herc is used to skepticism. As a black man, he has had to deal with it his entire life.

He looks himself over as they gaze at him open mouthed. "I am as mean as I look, but I'm on your side. This is my momma's blood, cause those bastards killed her. My shirt's ripped up from fightin' to save my family. I stood guard on your roadblock, as asked, and I'm willing to run convoy to Central City. So quit lookin' at the black man like he's crazy. I'm on your side!"

Stunned silence is replaced by some laughs and a few quick introductions. The tension has been relieved. Herc lets them know he knows where Mark's farm is. He asks about the trucker putting the convoy together, and they let him know where it is forming up. They let him know why they need to get information to Mark. It is him and his family that have a bounty on their heads.

Mark has helped Herc through many tough times, given him a chance when no one else would. And Herc has stood by Mark, worked hard, and been loyal. Herc will not let this threat pass lightly.

***

Word comes through that several farms have been hit hard, starting the day before. The men killed, and the women gone. Livestock killed for no reason, but some of it taken. The random killings on the main roads have slowed down, but every once in a while a truck or a few bikes will pull up and pop off a few rounds. A few less well defended roadblocks have had satchel charges thrown at them, exploding violently. Three people have been killed in these roadblock attacks.

Nerves are on edge. People's families are out there where the savages are pillaging. The loss of the Fire Chief and the slaughter at the renegades' compound has had a chilling effect. Even with the defenses the town has set up, people feel helpless. The convoy to Central City is a rallying call, a way to establish some control. It is decided that four trucks and a few off-road bikes will make up the convoy. That many trucks are needed to help take people back to their homes. That many people have been stranded in town. Some people want to be dropped off at their homes, some have made it clear that they want to pick up their families and bring them back to town, to safety. The bikes are to move fast and act as a forward patrol. Herc is in the second truck in line. They are to go all the way to Central City, along with the truck behind them. He is riding shotgun, Leesa and John Jr. are in the back of the truck. Sandbags have been laid along the sides of the bed to give them some protection.

A few miles out of town their scout reports back that there is a farm on fire ahead of them. They had stopped to check it out, and heard gunfire. The leader of the convoy has them move forward at top speed hoping to help this farmer that may still be under attack. Their timing is almost perfect, almost. They see a bike heading away from them as they turn a bend in the road. They crest a hill and see a farmhouse on fire, two trucks heading out of the drive led by the bike. There are several people running about the farmyard, emerging from fighting positions, shooting at the retreating raiders.

The convoy pulls in the drive, and cheers go up from the farmstead. But the attention is quickly turned to the house that is fully engulfed in flames. It is quickly determined that the house is lost, but that the out buildings need to be saved. The men and women in the convoy begin to try to save the out buildings and barn, some start to attend to a woman and child, burned and wounded in the raid.

A raider party had been stopped, five lives saved. The convoy leader offers them a ride to Central City, but they are pissed and determined. An abandoned house trailer on the property will be their new home. They are not leaving their farm, their land. The convoy spends over an hour at the farmstead. Herc has them set up security first, then they proceed to evaluating and helping as they can, getting the story of what happened.

It is mid-afternoon by the time they head out. A strong thunderstorm rolls through as they make the last few miles to Central City. They see some houses that look abandoned. They see some farms clearly being defended, even a few tractors out harvesting corn and hay. They drop a few people off at their homes and farms. A truck stops at a doctor's home, and his wife and kids are picked up. They all head back to the safety of Hooversville. Another truck peals off at a country road to take a wife and kids to a home they have not seen in three days. Finally, late that afternoon, what is left of the convoy rolls up on a serious roadblock just outside of Central City.

The convoy stops short of the roadblock, and as the two parties meet, hugs are exchanged, some tears are shed. The convoy is passed through and led to a large church parking lot. There the scene is controlled chaos. Stragglers hope for a way forward. A few people of authority, including some vets forming a civilian army, are pumping the convoy crew for information. Many people just want news, news from the rest of the world, news from their neighbors, news from a cousin or brother; has Hooversville been attacked by the savages, have they heard from any other towns? The questions come in floods.

A tall wiry man, with a stern face but bright eyes, steps into the crowd that has formed around the convoy. "Calm down, people, calm down. Let's welcome our guests with some food and water. Let's give them some space." His commanding voice quiets the crowd, and they start to move back. One straggler continues to demand to be heard, and questions the newcomers, but a stern look from the tall man sends him back to his group, under a pop-up pavilion at the edge of the large parking lot.

The tall wiry man continues to politely separate the convoy people from the rest of the townsfolk and stragglers. He and a strongly built squat man, with some tattoos on his arm, manage to get the newcomers aside. Several other people with military bearing are helping to keep people calm and organized.

The tall man addresses the people from the convoy. "I'm John Fisher. I seem to have been pressed back into my country's service, due to the present circumstances. I have been asked by some prominent local folks to help us through this current situation. The situation I refer to is not just the power outage, but the raiding going on by the anarchists. It's a wonder that you have made it here! These barbarians have been shooting up the roads, looting and killing.

"I pulled you all aside, so we can hear what's going on out there. We need to stop these bastards. Just so you all know, I'm a retired First Sergeant form the 101st Airborne Division. My friend here has eight years of Marine Corps service and there are many other vets here who are looking to set things right, to stop the violence. So you all convoyed up here from Hooversville? I want to hear what's going on, how you got here."

Eight people begin talking at once, fire chief killed, ambushes, pharmacy raided, farms raided. In a loud but calm voice, John quiets them all down. "Who is in charge of the convoy?" The trucker steps forward. John proceeds to debrief him, and the entire group, including Herc. The picture painted is one of chaos, but there are bright spots. The towns are organizing and it seems the barbarians have been dealt a few set backs. That the barbarians seem to have C4 explosives and a M60 machine gun is alarming. The death of Fire Chief Speigle is more alarming, along with the attached note.

Forty-five minutes later, the group disperses. Herc looks around for his girl and boy, wondering what comes next. He still needs to make it to Mark's farm. Despite all the efforts of the locals to normalize things, he is surrounded by chaos, rumors and panic. He can't even find the guy who said he would get him to Mark's farm. He feels a tug at his arm and turns to see the squat Marine vet.

"You been through a lot to get here. You're quiet, but you know more and have seen more than you're saying. Top, I mean John, would like to talk to you some more. We may want you to help us out in beating back these meth heads." They talk a bit more as the Marine leads him to where John has set up a command post. The Marine points out where Leesa and John Jr. are being fed and taken care of by another member of the paramilitary group. They exchange a wave and a wink.

At Sergeant Fisher's impromptu CP, welcoming exchanges are made. The First Seargent, also known as Top, asks in more detail about what went on in Moxham and the two gun battles there. Herc cries as he relates the grief of the loss of his parents and brother once again, but his determination and grit are laid bare as well, as he describes his journey this far. Top stays stoic through the tale, but is disturbed at the extent that Johnstown has fallen into chaos. He also inquires more deeply into Herc's relationship with Mark Mays. Top ends up convinced that Herc is a true man, looking out for his family and friends, and also a dangerous man, one he needs as an ally.

"The note, with the threat against Mark, one of the drivers brought it with him. It needs to be taken seriously. We have heard others who have survived raids talk about the barbarians asking about the guy in the old green and white van with the trailer. That's your boss, that's Mark. He fought back against them first, and his group killed this barbarian's boys. These threats are serious. We need to let him know, and we need to help him out. I've heard about how he started helping the town get ready, from day one, for the chaos we now see. That kind of foresight and generosity cannot be forgotten."

The day is starting to get late, and storm clouds are brewing to the west, dark thunder clouds billowing from the heat and humidity of the early fall day. Herc agrees to take Top and a few other men in a two truck convoy the few miles out to Mark's farm. They hurry to try and beat the storm. Top issues a few orders to his paramilitary group before he loads up for the trip out to the farmstead.

Twenty minutes later, the rainstorm catches up to the small convoy as they slow to turn onto the country lane that leads back to the farmstead. They hear a loud bell ringing in the distance, as they pass the vacant house on the corner of the county road and the country lane. Herc hollers for them to stop. "Mark ain't no dumb ass, he knows we're here." He yells over the storm raging around them. "Top, you and me better walk in from here."

The two trucks stop fifty yards off the county road, the abandoned house to their right and cornfields on their left. The lane goes straight over a rise and nothing else can be seen. The rain begins to come down in torrents as lightning strikes nearby. The wind whips the cornfields and distant trees. "How can he know we're here? There's nothing here. Where are we headed to anyway?" The First Sergeant begins to look a Herc suspiciously.

"You hear that bell? You think it's recess time?" Herc responds indigjantly. "I don't know how he knows, but he knows. Maybe a scout in the field, or someone in a tree. Mark is no dumb ass. He got a sweet setup back there, and he won't let that go without a fight. Let's just walk back, and see what's up. He's a good guy, trust me on this. We roll up with two trucks of armed men and women, and we'll be walking into a gun battle."

John thinks for a bit, looks at Herc, and then nods his head. "Everything I've heard about this guy, he is different. That bell is ringing for a reason. Okay, lets' walk up and see what's going on. But I am not walking up there unarmed."

"You walk up there unarmed, and he'll think it's a trap. I'm going up there armed, and he's my best friend in the world right now. Besides that, I work for him. If I show up unarmed, he'll probably bitch at me for not being ready to go to work!" Herc laughs at his own joke, which goes over Top's head. "You got a white flag to wave, an old rag or a bandana?" They find an old rag and Herc ties it to his 30/30. He lets Leesa know they are walking in, as the first sergeant talks with his guys. Herc again reassures them that it is all good. The bell has stopped ringing by this time, but the rain and thunder continue.

Soaked to the bone, the tall stern white man, and the shorter stocky black man head down the muddy gravel lane, soon engulfed by eight foot high corn stalks on either side. A few hundred yards down the narrow lane, the outlines of the old farmhouse come into view. As they top a rise in the road, they see the big Dodge truck blocking the lane. Herc raises the white flag higher, and waves it back and forth. He asks John to put his hands up as they walk the final few hundred yards to the small roadblock. The farmhouse becomes more distinct through the heavy rain as they get closer. A loud and commanding voice bellows from the farmhouse. "Halt and state your business."

Herc, knowing the loud voice, hollers back. "It's Herc, and a friend, Mark. I got Leesa and John Jr. with me. This guy is an Army Ranger, he's helped me get here." They see movement on the porch. They wait a bit.

"Herc? Is that you?" responds the loud voice from the porch.

"Yessiree, boss! Alive and well! Got a friend with me and more in some trucks on the road."

"You and your friend, come on up. The trucks have to stay where they are for now."

The rain has already started to slow down, and the sky is growing lighter. The farmhouse comes more fully into view. Top and Herc approach the house, walking around the truck parked broadside in the lane. As they round the front bumper of the truck, Mark runs off the porch and gives Herc a huge bear hug, not a man hug, a full blown loving hug. Herc hugs him back. Both get a little teary eyed as they step back, and eye each other up.

"I can't believe you're here! I saw Moxham on fire, I saw the chaos! Oh my God! Praise the Lord!" Mark hugs his faithful employee of fifteen years again, more tears welling in his eyes. "Let's get out of this rain, come up on the porch." Mark beckons them to follow him.

Up on the porch, Ken, Linc and Larson are at ready arms, behind their new sandbagged firing positions. Mark tells them to stay alert, as introductions are made. "First Sergeant, huh? Back in my day, you would be called Top. That still a tradition?" The First Sergeant grins and nods.

Top and Herc are both impressed with the fortifications they had made just that day. Mark questions Sergeant Fisher, gets his background, and why he is there. He is satisfied that all is good, and allows for them to bring their two trucks in, but they are not to be allowed in the house, or to roam the property. Herc sprints back to the trucks, and his family, to let them know they can come on up.

The First Sergeant is a little miffed at Mark's restrictions, and Mark can tell. "John, this is my property, and it is none of your business what is on my property. I just met you, and I will consider you a friend. I will help you in anyway I can, but you have to live by my rules on my property. Times have changed. I can't trust any stranger walking on to my land with free range to see what we may have, and how we are defended. You have to understand that. You can see that we are not helpless. We can be an ally, but I must look after my family first. Would you allow a stranger and his group to roam freely around your headquarters, see your defenses, your supplies?" John nods in understanding, seeing that he is dealing with someone who has common sense and military tact.

"Britt," I holler, "Bring up some sandwiches from the rest of that bread you made today. And have Becca bring up some cider." I hear her moving from the upstairs, and head out the back door.

"You drink bourbon, Top?"

"I wouldn't mind wetting my lips." His stern look softens a bit as he sees our hospitality towards them is genuine.

"Ken, bring out a bottle of Maker's Mark, not the cheap stuff, Okay? Bring some glasses, too." Ken looks at me warily, as he turns towards the door. I nod at him trying to indicate that it's okay. He is understandably wary, with two truckloads of armed men coming down the driveway.

By the time the two trucks get to our roadblock, the late summer storm has passed. Leesa, Herc and John Jr. jump out with their meager belongings and come up on the porch, wide eyed. We exchange hugs. Janie points out a few comfortable chairs for them. She tries to get them to talk with her, but they are exhausted and in a bit of shock. She offers them water and tells them food is on the way, trying to comfort them, welcome them.

Ken returns with some glasses and a prized bottle of bourbon. He pours two glasses, two fingers each, and returns to his ready position. "Herc, you care for some Maker's Mark, too?" I ask looking at where he is sitting, and beckoning him over. His eyes brighten.

"Yessiree, boss!" he exclaims, He tries to make a quick and agile move to join us, but fails miserably. He laughs at himself. "Been a tough few days, Mark, ain't moving as fast as I'd like." He shuffles over as I pour another two-finger glass.

I look at Top and Herc as I raise my glass, "Here's to new friends, and long journeys." We all take a good strong sip. "So what's going on in Central City, since I left yesterday? Things seemed to be starting to shape up."

"I understand you helped initiate some of the programs to move the stragglers through and to beef up the roadblocks. I have to thank you for that," says Top. "I came on the scene yesterday, soon after the meth head turncoat and his girlfriend showed up. We've been gathering vets and other strong men and women to put together a militia, for lack of a better term. The meth heads have quieted down a bit, but are still causing problems, especially outside of town. Farms are getting hit, as is anyone on the roads, unless they are in a convoy. And our roadblocks have been harassed. Your man showed up on a convoy from Hooversville. They took a serious hit this morning. Two renegades came in fast, backed up by some serious firepower and managed to throw two satchel charges at one of their roadblocks. Two young men got killed, and they blew two trucks to bits. They also rolled up and dropped a message for us, or more to the point, for you."

"Huh, what do the meth heads want with me?"

"Seems you and yours killed two of their leader's sons. They put a bounty on your head. They want you dead."

THE END OF BOOK1, RIGHTEOUS GATHERING

Final words

I hope you enjoyed reading this novel. It is the first book in this new series, "Righteous Survival, an EMP Saga." Book two is well over halfway written and takes Mark, Becca, and the rest of their family and community further into the mounting chaos. As one situation is dealt with, more arise. The societal chaos and reset of the American way of life continues. I expect the next book to be available by late winter or early spring of 2017.

I want to thank Steph, Kim, Erica, Wes, Phil, Maren, Ruby, Barb and Linc for their help and feedback in the process of writing the novel.

As an independent author, I am not under the constraints of a demanding publisher, which increases my creative parameters. But I do not have the marketing power of the publishing houses. Reviews are what drives demand. Please write and sumbit an honest review.

Made in the USA
Lexington, KY
06 April 2017